THE
FUSS-FREE
FAMILY
COOKBOOK

THE FUSS-FREE FAMILY COOKBOOK

No More Separate Meals for Adults and Children

CIARA ATTWELL

Lagom

For Aoife & Fintan

CONTENTS

INTRODUCTION

It has been nine years since I first started sharing recipes online and it's safe to say that the way in which I cook and the type of recipes I make has changed and evolved as the years have gone by. My children are now eleven and nine. The weaning years are long gone, the fussy toddler stages have passed, and I'm now at a place where I aim to cook just one meal for the whole family.

Although their eating habits have improved over time, my children are still not always the most adventurous of eaters and would gladly have the same few dinners every week! I'm still working on developing their taste buds and introducing them to new flavours all the time, balancing this with my own meals to ensure that I'm not making separate food for everyone. This is really important to me, and I know to a lot of other parents as well, because we are all short of time. Not making separate meals every day, up to three times a day, means we can save so much more in terms of budget, too.

My own eating habits have also evolved in the past couple of years. I've spent years working to help parents feed their children good, home-cooked, healthy food but, behind the scenes, I wasn't doing that for myself. By the summer of 2020, just as we started to come out of the first lockdown, I felt completely burnt out. I was mentally and physically exhausted like every other parent balancing homeschooling and working. I knew I couldn't control the global situation happening at the time, but what I could control was my own health and well-being.

I set about making some realistic changes to my lifestyle; moving more, sleeping better and, most noticeably, unpacking the food that I was eating. There was no particular 'diet' that I followed. I have a long history of yo-yo dieting, jumping on whatever is the latest weight-loss trend. This time, I ignored all that and instead concentrated on cooking healthy but hearty recipes. I became more mindful of the calories in food (but never fully tracked them) and set myself a daily limit. I wanted this to be a long-term lifestyle change rather than a quick-fix solution. I was also conscious of not creating any kind of diet culture in our house. As we were all eating the same food, my children never knew that I was actively making changes. This was really important to me, especially raising a pre-teen daughter. Over the next eighteen months, I lost 60lbs eating the most delicious food and not depriving myself of treats or snacks.

As I started to share this journey online, I received hundreds of messages from other parents and carers in the same position. They were putting so much time and energy into their children's health and eating habits, but not looking after themselves in the same way. With this book I want to bridge that gap; creating recipes that are healthy and nutritious for us adults but suitable for the whole family, too.

In short, this is not a diet book! I won't tell you how many calories you should be eating every day or give you a list of foods to avoid. But what I want to give you is one hundred delicious breakfast, lunch, dinner and snack recipes that are nutritionally balanced and perfect for adults and kids alike.

Some of the serving suggestions can be tweaked for adults and children and I have also included a chapter on delicious lower calorie salads and sides to bulk out the main meals.

Cooking good, nutritious food for the whole family doesn't have to be stressful or difficult, and I really hope these recipes help make your time in the kitchen, and time spent eating as a family, as enjoyable as possible.

Ciara
xx

@myfussyeater

ABOUT THIS BOOK

This cookbook contains one hundred recipes broken down into seven chapters. The recipes are all designed to be fuss free: easy-to-source ingredients, using minimal equipment, with clear and simple instructions.

BREAKFAST

Whether you enjoy a sweet or savoury breakfast, this chapter will give you lots of inspiration to kickstart your day. Some recipes can be made in advance to save time on busy mornings. Others are best made fresh and perfect for slower weekend starts. There are also options that can be packed up and taken to work.

LUNCH & LIGHT MEALS

Say goodbye to boring sandwiches! This chapter will give you ideas from pasta salads and fritters, to bagels, wraps and toasties. These recipes can also work as a lighter evening meal or be bulked up with recipes from the Salads & Sides chapter.

WEEKDAY MEALS

Cooking for a family mid-week can often be stressful. Between school runs, activity drop-offs and your own home and work schedule, there is often little time and headspace for long and complicated evening meals. These recipes can all be whipped up in 30 minutes or less. Think kid-friendly pastas, tasty burgers and speedy noodle dishes that the whole family can enjoy!

WEEKEND MEALS

Weekend meals are just that: dinners to make at the weekend or on days when you have more time to devote to cooking. These recipes require a little more prep and cooking time than the speedy mid-week meals, but are still all easy to follow using everyday ingredients.

SOUPS, STEWS & CASSEROLES

Some days you just need a big bowl of comfort food, and these recipes will do the trick. Make them for lunch or dinner, with options to bulk them out for a heartier meal. Some of the soup recipes also make great pasta sauces for fussy eating children.

SALADS & SIDES

The recipes in this chapter are designed to complement main meals. Add lots of nutrient-dense sides to adult dinners with simple but delicious salads, and there's kid-friendly recipes too like cheesy garlic bread and easy homemade naan.

SNACKS & DESSERTS

Whether you're looking for ideas to batch make for afternoon snacks or a weekend dessert recipe, the whole family can enjoy my healthier twists on these sweet treats.

HOW TO USE THIS BOOK

AGE RANGE

All the recipes in this book are suitable for children from age two upwards. Some recipes contain ingredients such as salt and honey etc. which are not suitable for weaning babies. You can, however, adapt these recipes to make them so. I am always available on my social media accounts to chat through any adaptations you want to make, so feel free to message me.

SERVING SUGGESTIONS

Lots of the recipes contain different serving suggestions for adults and children. For example, I may suggest a side salad for adults and chopped crudités such as carrots and cucumbers for children. Obviously, this is just a guide and feel free to adapt the serving suggestions depending on what foods your family enjoy.

Some recipes will also suggest different ways to plate up the food for children to make it more visually appealing to them.

Some of the things I think about include making sure favourite plates, bowls and cutlery are clean each day, so they can be a familiar source of food. Having a supply of edible decorations for desserts and cakes, having different-coloured foods in separate sections of the plate, providing a meal with toppings kids can add themselves – all of these things have helped me out over the years. I have a cupboard full of cutlery and crockery that sometimes make mealtimes more fun and appealing.

SWAPS & SUBSTITUTIONS

I have included the below icons in each recipe so you can easily see if a recipe contains the main food allergens. However, most of the recipes can be easily adapted with alternatives such as gluten-free flour, dairy-free yogurt etc. Again, I am always happy to chat through specific food swaps on social media.

GF	GLUTEN FREE
DF	DAIRY FREE
EF	EGG FREE
NF	NUT FREE
V	VEGETARIAN

LOW-FAT INGREDIENTS

In many of my recipes I use lower-fat ingredients such as fat-free Greek yogurt, Lighter than Light mayonnaise, semi-skimmed milk etc. Full-fat dairy is always recommended for children under two years of age as their energy and growing requirements rely on the calories in these products. According to current NHS and government guidance, it is fine to give lower-fat alternatives to children. If you would prefer to use full-fat versions of anything, that is absolutely fine. It won't alter the taste in any way.

Personally, when a recipe states to serve ingredients such as yogurt on the side (rather than in the recipe itself), then I always use a full-fat version for my children and a fat-free or lower-fat version for myself. This, however, is entirely up to you!

PORTION SIZES

The lunch and dinner recipes are all based on four portions and the calories have been calculated accordingly. If you have younger children with small appetites or older teenagers that eat larger portions, then you many want to adjust the quantities of the ingredients.

CALORIES

As I explained in the Introduction, I don't count calories or set myself any kind of target each day. I do believe it's important that we have a rough idea of the energy density of

the food that we are eating. It's easy to make assumptions about meals based on the way that they are described. I've seen salads on a restaurant menu with over 1,000 calories, but creamy pastas listed for just 500. I calculate the calories of my recipes when I first make them so that I can be mindful of my intake, without having to rely on tracking everything that I eat.

I have included the calorie counts of the recipes in this book for this very reason, but there is no goal, no limit and no requirement to track them yourself. It's important to remember that your body and your appetite are not exact machines. Some days we will feel hungrier than others, particularly for those with fluctuating monthly cycles. On hungrier days, choose some of the higher calorie recipes or eat a larger portion. Ensure you are eating enough protein as well as filling up on fruits and vegetables, but by all means eat that snack or treat that you are craving!

> ### A NOTE ON OILS:
> Unless stated otherwise, all oil used in recipes can be either olive oil or sunflower oil.

INGREDIENT ESSENTIALS

These are some of the ingredients that I always have in my kitchen and use consistently throughout this book. I have tried to use a lot of the same ingredients in many different recipes to avoid waste and cut down on shopping costs. If you have leftover ingredients from one recipe, then check out the Index at the back of this book as it will tell you the other recipes that use the same ones.

STORE CUPBOARD ESSENTIALS:

Herbs & Spices

Garlic powder

Onion powder

Dried Oregano

Dried Thyme

Smoked paprika

Mild curry powder

Mild curry paste

Mild chilli powder

Ground Cumin

Dried Goods

Stock pots or stock cubes

Microwave rice

Long grain rice

Spaghetti and pasta shapes

Orzo

Egg, rice and ramen noodles

Plain and self-raising flour

Cornflour

Baking powder

Bicarbonate of soda

Porridge oats

Cocoa powder

Golden breadcrumbs

Panko breadcrumbs

Tins, Jars & Bottles

Lighter than Light mayonnaise

Chilli sauce

Tinned tomatoes

Tomato purée

Chickpeas

Butter beans

Tinned sweetcorn

Honey

Peanut butter

Soy sauce

Olive oil

Sunflower oil

Spray oil

Vanilla extract

Dijon mustard

Fresh Fruit & Vegetables

Carrots

Cucumber

Tomatoes

Cherry tomatoes

Peppers

Potatoes

Spring onions

Celery

Courgette

Sugar snap peas

Baby spinach

Lettuce

Apples

Bananas

Pears

Berries

Lemons

Limes

Oranges

Fridge

Semi-skimmed milk

Butter

Fat-free Greek yogurt

Full-fat Greek yogurt

Cheddar cheese

Parmesan cheese

Sliced cheese

Eggs

Freezer

Frozen diced onions

Frozen chopped garlic

Frozen chopped ginger

Mixed frozen vegetables

Frozen peas

Frozen sweetcorn

Frozen fruit

FUSSY EATERS

I know only too well the stress that fussy eating can put on families. We all just want our children to eat well, get the right balance of nutrients and enjoy a wide variety of food. In addition, social media can put a lot of pressure on parents when it seems that everyone else's children are lapping up every dish served to them, and even choose broccoli as a snack!

But, believe me, that is not the case. My children's eating has improved over the years, but not a day goes by when I don't hear 'yuck' or 'I'm not eating that'. It's something I still have to work on and I imagine I still will be well into their teen years.

Every child is individual, and their tastes and appetites all develop at different stages. All you can do is your best when working on their eating habits and try not to get too stressed about it. However, if you are particularly worried about their diet or your child has an extremely selective list of foods that they will eat, then I would always advise seeking professional help.

For moderately picky eaters, these are some tips that you might find helpful.

SMALL PORTIONS & FOOD COMBINING

Large plates of food can be overwhelming for most children, let alone fussy eaters. Start with small meals and snacks – they can always ask for more if they are enjoying it. Food combining has also worked well for my children. Many of the recipes in this book were very new tastes and flavours for my children. I offered them a small portion to start with, along with something small that I know they will enjoy, like a sandwich.

80/20 RULE

When introducing new foods, I usually recommend the 80/20 rule. Aim for 80 per cent of the plate to be foods they know and love. If you give them a whole plate of new foods, they are more likely to become anxious and instantly refuse it. It will help stop the overwhelm as they recognise foods that they already eat. They will most likely begin with eating their favourite elements of the meal and, with some encouragement, may try the new foods.

FRONT LOADING

When offering new foods, pick a time of the day when children are less tired and more relaxed. This is particularly true for younger children. During the week, when they've had a full day at school or nursery, and perhaps after school clubs, they are physically and mentally tired and don't always have the capacity to try new foods.

Instead, shift the focus to trying new foods earlier in the day, like at breakfast and lunch. Weekends are also a great time to try new foods when everyone is rushing that little bit less.

GET THEM INVOLVED

Getting the kids involved in food preparation and shopping is a great way to pique their interest in what they are actually eating.

Most children love baking cookies and cakes and that's a great start. But also get them to help chop fruit and veggies whilst you are cooking (obviously, with supervision). Giving children their own shopping list at the supermarket is another trick that I use!

For older children, let them look through cookbooks or recipe websites and encourage them to choose some meals for the week ahead that they think look good.

NO GOOD OR BAD FOODS

This is a principle I've been trying to adopt with my kids for the past couple of years. I never want to demonise any particular food. Everything has its place in our diets. There are foods we eat more of and more regularly, and other foods that we can enjoy in moderation.

This is the reason I often serve sweet treats alongside savoury meals. Snacks and desserts are not something that need to be earned by the child for eating their dinner, and it stops us as adults bribing a child to eat their meal with the promise of something sweet afterwards.

When trying this method, you may find that your child instantly reaches for the sweet element first. Don't worry, this is perfectly normal! Allow them to choose the order in which they eat. If you are worried about them filling up and not eating their main meal, then start with just a small portion of the sweet food on their plate first.

REINTRODUCE LITTLE AND OFTEN

When our children refuse a particular food or meal, we often dismiss it instantly and assign it to the reject pile. Children's taste buds are developing all the time and something they hated last month may actually be more appealing to them this month. Remember to keep trying with new foods and think of other ways to serve it to them (I'll include some of my top tips throughout the book). For meals that are rejected, try freezing a small portion and defrosting, heating up and re-serving it another day. It means less waste and less work for you too.

BREAKFAST

French Toast Crumpets
Ham & Cheese Croissants
Banana Orange Breakfast Muffins
Breakfast Bagels
Banana Breakfast Fritters
Bacon & Cheese Flatbreads
Chocolate Protein Shake
Strawberry Scones
Mexican Scramble Tacos
Chocolate Cherry Bircher
Chocolate Granola Parfait
Cheat's Egg Florentine
Strawberry & White Chocolate Baked Oats
Lemon & Poppy Seed Overnight Oats
Pesto Eggs with Roasted Veggies
Breakfast Boxes

FRENCH TOAST CRUMPETS

| Serves: 4 | Prep time: 5 minutes | Cook time: 10 minutes | Calories: 310 per portion |

Upgrade basic crumpets to a more exciting breakfast! These are great to serve up to children who don't usually eat eggs.

INGREDIENTS

6 crumpets
2 medium eggs
100ml semi-skimmed milk
1 tbsp honey
1 tsp vanilla extract
1 tbsp butter

To serve:
500g fat-free Greek yogurt
150g mixed fresh berries

SERVING SUGGESTIONS:

Serve with Greek yogurt and mixed fresh berries, or spread on some Nutella, jam or peanut butter for little mouths.

STORING:

These crumpets are best eaten immediately after cooking.

METHOD

1. Cut the crumpets in half across the middle.

2. Add the eggs, milk, honey and vanilla extract to a wide bowl and mix well.

3. Dip six of the crumpet halves into the egg mixture, first bottom side down, then turn them over and leave them to soak up the mixture for 30 seconds.

4. Melt the butter in a frying pan on the hob.

5. Add the six crumpet halves, top side down and cook for 3 minutes.

6. Turn them over and cook for another 2 minutes.

7. In the meantime, repeat the process with the remaining six halves.

8. When the first batch of crumpets are cooked, remove from the pan and set aside and cook the remaining six.

HAM & CHEESE CROISSANTS

| Serves: 4 | Prep time: 3 minutes | Cook time: 4 minutes | Calories: 290 per croissant |

Savoury croissants feel like an indulgent treat, but it's easy to make them a little healthier at home for a tasty and filling breakfast.

INGREDIENTS

4 small croissants

2 tbsp Lighter than Light mayonnaise

½ tsp Dijon mustard

2 tomatoes

8 slices (100g) wafer ham

4 slices (100g) edam cheese

SERVING SUGGESTIONS:

For a light breakfast, serve with chopped fresh fruit. For a more substantial breakfast, serve with a baked hash brown and sliced avocado. Choose as appropriate for children too, and even sprinkle some more cheese on top for extra protein.

STORING:

These croissants are best eaten immediately after cooking.

METHOD

1. Cut the croissants open so that they lie flat but don't cut all the way.

2. Mix the mayonnaise and Dijon mustard together in a small bowl and then spread a little on both sides of the croissant.

3. Slice the tomatoes and add them to the open croissant along with the ham and cheese.

4. Place the croissant open under the grill for 3-4 minutes until the cheese has melted.

5. Close the croissant and serve immediately.

BANANA ORANGE BREAKFAST MUFFINS

| Serves: 10 | Prep time: 6 minutes | Cook time: 25 minutes | Calories: 180 per muffin |

These fruity muffins are brilliant to make in advance for a quick mid-week breakfast.

INGREDIENTS

200g plain flour

75g porridge oats, plus 1 tbsp to top

1 tsp baking powder

¼ tsp bicarbonate of soda

50g butter, melted

150g fat-free plain yogurt

1 medium egg

50g honey

1 banana, mashed

zest and juice of 1 orange

SERVING SUGGESTIONS:

Serve with Greek yogurt and chopped fresh fruit for adults and kids. You can cut fruit into different shapes using cookie cutters, and let kids serve their yogurt themselves.

STORING:

These muffins will keep in an airtight container for up to 3 days and can be reheated in the microwave. They can be frozen for up to 3 months and defrosted at room temperature in 2–3 hours.

METHOD

1. Preheat the oven to 180°C Fan/200°C/ Gas Mark 6.

2. Add the plain flour, porridge oats, baking powder and bicarbonate of soda to a large bowl and mix with a spoon.

3. Add the melted butter, yogurt, egg, honey, mashed banana and the zest and juice of the orange to another bowl or jug and mix well.

4. Add the wet ingredient to the dry ingredients and mix again just enough until the ingredients are well combined.

5. Divide the mixture between 10 silicone muffin cases. I find it easier to do this with an ice-cream scoop. One scoop of the mixture fits a muffin case perfectly.

6. Top the muffins with a sprinkling of the additional oats.

7. Bake in the oven for 22–25 minutes.

8. Once cooked, remove from the oven and leave to cool for a few minutes before taking the muffins out of the cases.

BREAKFAST BAGELS

| Serves: 4 | Prep time: 4 minutes | Cook time: 12 minutes | Calories: 365 per portion |

Forget plain toast or boring cereal, this is one of my favourite weekend breakfasts to make – and the whole family love them too!

INGREDIENTS

4 chicken sausages (260g)

spray oil

60g grated Cheddar cheese

4 medium eggs

4 bagel thins

SERVING SUGGESTIONS:

For a light breakfast, serve with chopped fresh fruit. For a more substantial breakfast, serve with a baked hash brown and sliced avocado.

For younger children, you may want to serve this meal deconstructed to make it easier for them to eat.

STORING:

These bagels are best eaten immediately after cooking.

METHOD

1. Remove the skins from the sausages and form each sausage into a thin patty.

2. Add some spray oil to a frying pan on the hob and cook the patties on a medium heat on one side for 4 minutes.

3. Turn and cook for a further 3 minutes.

4. Add the grated cheese to the top of the patties, cover with a lid and continue to cook for a final 1 minute.

5. When the patties are cooked, remove from the pan and set aside.

6. Crack the eggs into the same pan and cook for 3-4 minutes or longer if you prefer a firmer yolk.

7. Toast the bagel thins in the toaster. Add the patties to the bagel thins topped with a fried egg.

BANANA BREAKFAST FRITTERS

| Serves: 4 | Prep time: 5 minutes | Cook time: 16 minutes | Calories: 225 with toppings |

This recipe is a cross between a fritter and a pancake. The chunky banana pieces give an interesting texture and bite to the fritters, and they're really filling too.

INGREDIENTS

100g plain flour

1 tsp baking powder

½ tsp ground cinnamon

1 medium egg

100ml semi-skimmed milk

2 tbsp honey

2 bananas

½ tbsp butter

To serve:

200g fat-free Greek yogurt

8 strawberries

METHOD

1. Add the flour, baking powder and cinnamon to a large bowl and mix well.

2. Add the egg, milk and honey and mix again.

3. Chop the bananas into small pieces and mix into the fritter batter.

4. Melt the butter in a large frying pan.

5. Add a large spoonful of the fritter mixture to the pan at a time. You should be able to make eight fritters from this recipe, but you may have to cook them in two batches.

6. Cook on a low heat for 3-4 minutes on either side.

SERVING SUGGESTIONS:

Serve topped with the Greek yogurt and chopped strawberries for everyone.

STORING:

Fritters can be kept in the fridge for up to 3 days and reheated by frying them again for 1 minute on either side. Freeze for up to 3 months and defrost at room temperature for 3 hours.

BACON & CHEESE FLATBREADS

| Serves: 4 | Prep time: 1 minute | Cook time: 12 minutes | Calories: 260 per portion |

You can't beat the combination of bacon and cheese for a delicious, savoury breakfast. Perfect for a weekend treat, but also quick enough to make on a weekday too.

INGREDIENTS

spray oil

8 smoked bacon medallions

4 slices (100g) Red Leicester cheese

4 small, folded flatbreads

SERVING SUGGESTIONS:

For a light breakfast, serve with chopped fresh fruit. For a more substantial breakfast, serve with a baked hash brown and sliced avocado or grilled tomatoes.

STORING:

These flatbreads are best eaten immediately after cooking.

METHOD

1. Add some spray oil to a large frying pan on the hob and cook the bacon medallions on a medium heat for 3-4 minutes on either side.

2. Remove the bacon and wipe the pan with some kitchen roll.

3. Place the bacon and cheese inside the flatbreads and then toast the flatbreads in the pan for 1-2 minutes on either side until the cheese has melted and the bread is crispy.

CHOCOLATE PROTEIN SHAKE

| Serves: 4 | Prep time: 2 minutes | Cook time: none | Calories: 315 calories per portion |

I know a lot of people don't actually enjoy eating early in the morning, but we all know how important a good breakfast is. This chocolate shake is packed with 24g of protein, ideal for filling you up without having to eat an overwhelming amount of food.

INGREDIENTS

1 litre semi-skimmed milk

400g fat-free Greek yogurt

4 tbsp smooth peanut butter

2 tbsp cocoa powder

2 tbsp honey

1 tbsp chia seeds

handful of ice

METHOD

1. Add all the ingredients to a blender and blitz until smooth.

SERVING SUGGESTIONS:

Serve immediately in tall glasses.

For children, I would serve this alongside another breakfast item. Think about the glass, too – is there one more suited to milkshake which you could use? The chia seeds can make the shake a little bitty, so feel free to leave them out of the kids' portion, then add and re-blend your portion. This shake can also be frozen into lolly moulds too, perfect for warmer days as snacks or desserts.

STRAWBERRY SCONES

| Makes: 9 | Prep time: 10 minutes | Cook time: 18 minutes | Calories: 195 per scone (not incl. toppings) |

These strawberry scones are another great batch recipe to make for breakfast and have on hand for busy mid-week mornings. They are more rustic than normal scones as I don't use a cutter, but it makes them really easy to whip up with minimal equipment.

INGREDIENTS

300g plain flour

50g white sugar

2 tsp baking powder

pinch of salt

50g cold butter

150ml semi-skimmed milk

1 medium egg

1 tsp vanilla extract

75g strawberries, chopped

SERVING SUGGESTIONS:

Serve plain or with butter and jam. For a more substantial breakfast, serve with a side of Greek yogurt and fresh fruit. Serve to kids plain and give them a choice of toppings.

STORING:

These scones will keep in an airtight container for up to 3 days and can be reheated in the microwave. They can be frozen for up to 3 months and defrosted at room temperature in 2–3 hours.

METHOD

1. Preheat the oven to 200°C Fan/220°C/Gas Mark 7 and line a baking tray with parchment paper.

2. Add the flour, sugar, baking powder and salt to a large bowl and mix well.

3. Cut the cold butter into small cubes and rub it into the flour mixture until you get a breadcrumb consistency.

4. Add the milk, egg and vanilla and mix again.

5. Finally, fold in the chopped strawberries.

6. Divide the dough into 9 equal pieces, then shape roughly into round scones. If you find the mixture very sticky, then add a little flour to your hand.

7. Place on the lined tray and bake for 15–18 minutes until the tops are starting to brown.

8. Allow to cool for a couple of minutes before serving.

MEXICAN SCRAMBLE TACOS

| Serves: 4 | Prep time: 4 minutes | Cook time: 9 minutes | Calories: 360 per portion |

Upgrade your usual scrambled eggs with this Mexican twist. The veggies add some extra nutrition but also bulk out the meal to make it even more filling.

INGREDIENTS

4 small tortilla wraps

8 medium eggs

50ml semi-skimmed milk

salt and pepper

spray oil

200g cherry tomatoes, diced

1 yellow pepper, diced

2 spring onions, diced

100g grated Cheddar cheese

To serve:

2 tsp chilli sauce

chopped fresh coriander

SERVING SUGGESTIONS:

For adults, serve with chopped fresh coriander and a drizzle of chilli sauce.

Kids may find it easier to eat the scrambled eggs served on their own and the tortilla wrap cut into triangles.

STORING:

These tacos are best served immediately after cooking.

METHOD

1. Add the tortilla wraps to a dry frying pan on the hob and cook for 1-1.5 minutes on either side until they are warmed through and just starting to get crispy. You may have to do these one at a time depending on the size of your pan.

2. Crack the eggs into a jug or bowl. Add the milk and a little salt and pepper and whisk with a fork.

3. Add a little spray oil to the same frying pan and allow it to heat up.

4. Add the whisked eggs but leave them untouched for 30 seconds before breaking them up and stirring. Cook for another 30 seconds.

5. Add the cherry tomatoes, pepper, spring onions and grated Cheddar and mix well.

6. Cook for another 2 minutes, stirring every few seconds.

7. Serve the scramble inside the tacos, folded in half.

CHOCOLATE CHERRY BIRCHER

| Serves: 4 | Prep time: 6 minutes | Cook time: none | Calories per portion: 260 |

Bircher muesli makes a simple and filling breakfast for the whole family.
Packed with grated fruit, it is easy to prep too.

INGREDIENTS

120g frozen pitted cherries

130g porridge oats

150g fat-free Greek yogurt

100ml semi-skimmed milk

1 tbsp honey

1 apple

1 pear

To serve:

100g fat-free Greek yogurt

25g milk chocolate, grated

METHOD

1. Add the frozen cherries to a bowl and microwave for 90 seconds until fully defrosted.

2. In a large bowl, mix together the oats, yogurt, milk and honey.

3. Grate the apple and pear and add that to the bowl.

4. Finally, add the defrosted cherries and any juices and mix again.

5. Divide into four bowls or glasses.

SERVING SUGGESTIONS:

Top with the Greek yogurt and grated chocolate, popping extra on for kids.

STORING:

Leftover Bircher muesli can be stored in the fridge for up to 2 days.

CHOCOLATE GRANOLA PARFAIT

| Makes: 10 portions | Prep time: 5 minutes | Cook time: 20 minutes | Calories: 320 per portion |

Busy morning? This is the one to make! The granola is nut-free to make it suitable for families with nut allergies, but feel free to add some mixed nuts if you like.

INGREDIENTS

For the granola:

250g porridge oats

50g mixed seeds

25g desiccated coconut

2 tbsp cocoa powder

60g unsalted butter

4 tbsp honey

1 tsp vanilla extract

For the coulis:

500g frozen mixed berries

2 tbsp honey

For the yogurt:

150g fat-free yogurt per portion

SERVING SUGGESTIONS:

Layer a portion each of the granola and coulis in a bowl or small jar with 150g of yoghurt. For kids, do more layers for an interesting variation.

STORING:

Store the granola in an airtight container at room temperature for up to 2 weeks. Store the coulis in an airtight container in the fridge for up to 4 days, or freeze for up to 3 months and defrost in the fridge overnight.

METHOD

1. Preheat the oven to 160°C Fan/180°C/ Gas Mark 4.

2. Add the oats, seeds, desiccated coconut and cocoa powder to a large bowl and mix well.

3. Add the butter to a jug and melt in the microwave.

4. Add the honey and vanilla to the melted butter and mix well.

5. Pour this into the bowl with the oats and mix until everything is well combined.

6. Divide between two baking trays and bake in the oven for 20 minutes.

7. Stir once or twice in this time as the edges will cook quicker than the rest.

8. Once cooked, remove from the oven and allow the granola to cool and crisp up on the trays.

9. To make the coulis, add the frozen berries to a large jug or bowl and cook in the microwave for 5-7 minutes until defrosted and heated through. You can also do this in a saucepan on the hob. Once cooked, stir in the honey.

10. The granola makes 10 x 40g portions and the coulis makes 10 x 50g portions.

CHEAT'S EGG FLORENTINE

| Serves: 4 | Prep time: 3 minutes | Cook time: 15 minutes | Calories: 350 per portion |

Egg Florentine is one of my top breakfast choices when I eat out. My version uses a cheat's hack instead of the usual hollandaise sauce for an easy homemade alternative.

INGREDIENTS

9 tbsp (135g) Lighter than Light mayonnaise

2 tsp English mustard

juice of ½ lemon

salt and pepper

½ tsp vinegar

8 medium eggs

4 English muffins

1 tsp butter

250g fresh baby spinach

SERVING SUGGESTIONS:

If you are worried that the mustard might be a bit overpowering for children, then just add a small drop to their sauce, then add some more when serving your own.

STORING:

This recipe is best eaten immediately after cooking.

METHOD

1. Make the cheat's hollandaise sauce by mixing together in a bowl the mayonnaise, English mustard, lemon juice and a little salt and pepper.

2. To poach the eggs, bring a large, shallow saucepan of water to just under boiling point, then turn down to a simmer and add a little salt and the vinegar. (To avoid overcrowding, cook four eggs at a time).

3. Crack one egg at a time into a small bowl or ramekin and gently pour into the water. Repeat with another three eggs.

4. Cook for 3 minutes for soft yolks or longer if you prefer them firmer.

5. Remove the eggs from the water with a slotted spoon and set aside on a plate.

6. Repeat the process with the remaining four eggs.

7. In the meantime, cut the muffins in half and toast in the toaster.

8. When the eggs are all poached, remove the water from the pan and rinse the saucepan.

9. Place the saucepan back on the heat with the butter and spinach. Cook for 1 minute until the spinach has softened. Season with salt and pepper.

10. Serve the muffins topped with some cooked spinach, a poached egg and finally the sauce spread on top.

11. You can add a little extra salt and pepper, if you wish, to the top of the egg.

STRAWBERRY & WHITE CHOCOLATE BAKED OATS

| Serves: 4 | Prep time: 4 minutes | Cook time: 30 minutes | Calories: 390 per portion |

Baked oats are a game-changer when it comes to easy breakfast prep. Simply mix all the ingredients together, pop into a dish and leave to bake for half an hour.

INGREDIENTS

spray oil

160g porridge oats

½ tsp baking powder

300g fat-free Greek yogurt

200ml semi-skimmed milk

2 medium eggs

2 tbsp honey

1 tsp vanilla extract

150g fresh strawberries, chopped

50g white chocolate chips

To serve:

200g fat-free Greek yogurt

50g fresh strawberries

METHOD

1. Preheat the oven to 180°C Fan/200°C/Gas Mark 6.

2. Spray a 26cm x 22cm baking dish with spray oil.

3. In a large bowl, mix together the porridge oats and baking powder.

4. Add the yogurt, milk, eggs, honey and vanilla and mix again.

5. Pour this mixture into the oiled dish.

6. Top with the chopped strawberries and white chocolate chips.

7. Bake in the oven for 30 minutes.

8. Serve immediately in bowls.

SERVING SUGGESTIONS:

Top with the extra Greek yogurt and chopped fresh strawberries. You could even grate a little bit more chocolate over the top for kids.

STORING:

Leftover baked oats can be stored in the fridge for up to 3 days and reheated in the oven or microwave. You may need to add a little extra milk if the oats have dried out.

LEMON & POPPY SEED OVERNIGHT OATS

| Serves: 4 | Prep time: 4 minutes | Cook time: minimum 2 hours in fridge | Calories: 250 per portion (not incl. toppings) |

Fresh and zesty, this overnight oats recipe is so easy to whip up the night before for a healthy and tasty breakfast in the morning.

INGREDIENTS

170g porridge oats

300g fat-free Greek yogurt

250ml semi-skimmed milk

zest and juice of 1 lemon

1 tbsp honey

1 tsp vanilla extract

1 tsp poppy seeds

METHOD

1. Add all the ingredients to a large bowl and mix well.

2. Cover and transfer to the fridge overnight or for a minimum of 2 hours.

SERVING SUGGESTIONS:

Transfer into individual bowls or pots and top with fresh berries, nuts, seeds or any other toppings of your choice. The same for children – give them the power to choose their toppings, and they are more likely to try what's underneath.

STORING:

Leftover overnight oats can be stored in the fridge for up to 3 days.

PESTO EGGS WITH ROASTED VEGGIES

| Serves: 4 | Prep time: 3 minutes | Cook time: 15 minutes | Calories: 250 per portion |

These pesto eggs were a viral foodie sensation last year, but I love them so much
I'm still eating them for breakfast now!

INGREDIENTS

200g baby mushrooms

200g cherry tomatoes

100g asparagus spears

spray oil

¼ tsp garlic powder

2 tbsp basil pesto

4 medium eggs

4 slices sourdough bread
(approx. 50g per slice)

SERVING SUGGESTIONS:

If your kids are not veggie fans,
you can swap theirs for a portion of
Greek yogurt and fresh fruit on
the side.

STORING:

This recipe is best served
immediately after cooking. Leftover
veggies however can be stored in
the fridge for up to 2 days.

METHOD

1. Preheat the oven to 180°C Fan/200°C/Gas Mark 6.

2. Add the baby mushrooms, cherry tomatoes and asparagus spears whole to a baking dish.

3. Spray on a little oil and add the garlic powder. Mix well.

4. Bake for 15 minutes.

5. In the meantime, add the pesto to a frying pan and spread it out around the pan.

6. Crack in the eggs and cook for 3-4 minutes or longer if you prefer the yolk to be fully set.

7. Toast the sourdough slices in a toaster.

8. Serve the pesto eggs on the slices of toasted sourdough with the roasted veggies on the side.

BREAKFAST BOXES

| Serves: 1 | Prep time: 4 minutes | Cook time: none | Calories: *see below* |

If you struggle to find the time to eat breakfast during the week, these breakfast boxes are perfect for you. Pack them up and take to the office or out and about to stop you getting ravenous by 11am. They can also be served up to kids at home who prefer picky bits for breakfast.

INGREDIENTS

Carbs:

1 small croissant

30g breadsticks

1 brioche

1 bagel thin

Protein & Fat:

20g cheese portion

1 boiled egg

1 cooked chicken sausage

50g hummus

150g low fat greek yogurt or high protein yogurt

Veg:

75g cherry tomatoes

50g cucumber

25g baby spinach

½ yellow or red pepper

Fruit:

4 strawberries

1 small apple

50g raspberries

40g blueberries

40g grapes

METHOD

1. Choose one food from Carbs, two from Protein & Fats, two portions of Veg and two portions of Fruit.

2. Pack into a lunchbox or Tupperware and eat within a couple of hours.

> **NOTES:**
>
> The calories in these Breakfast Boxes will depend on what ingredients you choose. The lowest the calories will be is 315 and the highest 480.

LUNCH & LIGHT MEALS

Chicken & Vegetable Sausage Rolls

Roasted Cauliflower Fritters with Fried Eggs

Coronation Chicken Salad

Croque Madame

Caprese Rice Salad

Bacon Mac & Cheese

Club Sandwich

Kimchi Cheese Toastie

Rainbow Veggie Wrap

Nasi Goreng

Chicken Caesar Pasta Salad

Melty Mozzarella Bagels

Crispy Tortilla Pizzas

Prosciutto Egg Muffins

Grazing Board Lunch

CHICKEN & VEGETABLE SAUSAGE ROLLS

| Serves: 4 | Prep time: 10 minutes | Cook time: 35 minutes | Calories: 320 for 3 sausages rolls |

My easy sausage roll recipe uses tortilla wraps instead of pastry for a healthier homemade version of this family favourite.

INGREDIENTS

spray oil

1 medium carrot

1 small courgette

1 red pepper

1 tsp oil

1 garlic clove, crushed

400g chicken sausages

2 large tortilla wraps

1 medium egg

1 tsp sesame seeds

STORING:

Leftover sausage rolls will keep in the fridge for up to 2 days and can be reheated in the oven.

Flash freeze before cooking, then bake from frozen, adding an extra 10 minutes to the cooking time.

METHOD

1. Preheat the oven to 200°C Fan/220°C/Gas Mark 7. Line a baking tray with parchment paper and spray with a little spray oil.

2. Finely grate the carrot and courgette and cut the pepper into very small, diced pieces.

3. Add 1 teaspoon of oil to a frying pan along with the veggies and garlic.

4. Cook on a low heat for 8–10 minutes until the pan is dry and there are no juices left from the courgette, stirring regularly.

5. Remove the skins from the sausages and add them to a large bowl. Add in the cooked veggies and mix well.

6. Place one of the tortilla wraps on a chopping board. Add half of the sausage and veggie mixture to the wrap, just right of the centre.

7. Starting on the right-hand side, roll the wrap up as tightly as you can, making sure that you finish seal side down. Cut off the ends of the wrap and then cut into six sausage rolls.

8. Place the individual sausage rolls on the lined baking tray and repeat the process with the other tortilla wrap.

9. Whisk the egg lightly in a cup and brush the tops and sides of the sausage rolls.

10. Sprinkle the sesame seeds on top and bake in the oven for 22–25 minutes until golden brown on top.

11. Serve immediately, three sausage rolls per person, with crudités or a side salad – good for everyone!

ROASTED CAULIFLOWER FRITTERS WITH FRIED EGGS

| Serves: 4 | Prep time: 5 minutes | Cook time: 40 minutes | Calories: 305 per portion |

Forget mushy boiled cauliflower, roast it instead for a more subtle and nutty flavour, then turn it into these delicious fritters the family will love.

INGREDIENTS

300g cauliflower
½ tbsp oil
¼ tsp garlic powder
100g plain flour
1 tsp baking powder
1 medium egg
100ml semi-skimmed milk
75g grated Cheddar cheese
2 tbsp chopped fresh chives
salt and pepper
spray oil

To top:
4 medium eggs

SERVING SUGGESTIONS:
For younger children, cut the fritters into finger-food-style slices and serve the fried egg on the side.

STORING:
Leftover fritters can be kept in the fridge for up to 3 days and reheated by frying them again for 1 minute on either side. They can be frozen for up to 3 months and defrosted at room temperature in 3 hours. The fried eggs are best made fresh.

METHOD

1. Preheat the oven to 200°C Fan/220°C/Gas Mark 7.

2. Chop the cauliflower into small florets and add to a baking dish with the oil and garlic powder. Mix well.

3. Bake for 20 minutes.

4. Add the flour, baking powder, egg and milk to a large bowl and mix well.

5. When the cauliflower is cooked, remove from the oven and chop into smaller pieces. Add the chopped cauliflower, grated cheese and chives to the fritter mixture and mix well. Season with a little salt and pepper.

6. Add some spray oil to a large frying pan.

7. Take a large spoonful of the fritter mixture and add it to the pan. The mixture will make eight fritters in total, but you will probably have to cook these in two batches.

8. Fry for 4 minutes on either side and set aside on a plate.

9. Add a little more spray oil to the pan and fry the eggs for 3–4 minutes, or longer if you prefer the yolk to be set.

10. Serve immediately, two fritters per portion topped with a fried egg.

CORONATION CHICKEN SALAD

| Serves: 4 | Prep time: 5 minutes | Cook time: none | Calories: 150 when served on lettuce leaves |

With a few simple tweaks, you can turn this British classic into a healthy light lunch.

INGREDIENTS

100g fat-free Greek yogurt

2 tbsp Lighter than Light mayonnaise

1 tbsp mango chutney

1 tbsp mild curry powder

½ tbsp chopped fresh chives

300g cooked chicken breast, chopped

salt and pepper

To serve:

2 heads little gem lettuce (for adults)

bread rolls (for children)

METHOD

1. Add the yogurt, mayonnaise, mango chutney and curry powder to a large bowl and mix well.

2. Add the chives and chopped chicken and mix again.

3. Season with a little salt and pepper.

SERVING SUGGESTIONS:

Serve in lettuce leaves for adults and on bread rolls or in a sandwich for children, along with a side salad or crudités.

STORING:

Leftovers can be kept in an airtight container in the fridge for up to 3 days.

CROQUE MADAME

This is my take on a French classic, served like an open sandwich for the ultimate comfort food lunch.

INGREDIENTS

4 slices (180g) sourdough bread

8 tbsp Lighter than Light mayonnaise

½ tbsp Dijon mustard

8 slices (60g) wafer-thin ham

4 large slices (100g) mature Cheddar cheese

spray oil

4 medium eggs

SERVING SUGGESTIONS:

Serve with a side salad or crudités. For younger children, you can slice the sourdough into more manageable pieces after grilling and add the egg on the side.

STORING:

This recipe is best eaten immediately after cooking.

METHOD

1. Toast the sourdough slices on one side under the grill. Turn the bread over but don't toast the other side.

2. Mix together the mayonnaise and Dijon mustard in a small bowl and spread this on the un-toasted side of the sourdough slices.

3. Add the slices of ham and then the cheese.

4. Pop back under the grill for 2–3 minutes until the cheese has melted.

5. In the meantime, add some spray oil to a frying pan and fry the eggs for 3–4 minutes or longer if you prefer the yolk to be set.

6. Serve the fried eggs on top of the sourdough.

CAPRESE RICE SALAD

| Serves: 4 | Prep time: 5 minutes | Cook time: 15 minutes | Calories: 385 per portion |

You can't beat the delicious flavours of mozzarella and basil. Mixed with cooked rice, this is a delicious light and summery lunch, perfect for picnics and BBQs too.

INGREDIENTS

For the salad:

300g long-grain rice

300g cherry tomatoes

125g mozzarella ball

handful fresh basil leaves

For the dressing:

1 tbsp olive oil

¼ tsp garlic powder

¼ tsp dried oregano

salt and pepper

METHOD

1. Bring a large saucepan of water to the boil on the hob.

2. Rinse the rice in a sieve under cold running water and add it to the saucepan.

3. Cook the rice according to the package instructions.

4. In the meantime, prep the rest of the ingredients. Cut the cherry tomatoes into halves or quarters and chop the mozzarella ball into bite-sized pieces.

5. Make the dressing by mixing the olive oil, garlic powder, oregano and a little salt and pepper together in a small bowl.

6. When the rice is cooked, drain it into a sieve. Run under cold water to cool the rice down.

7. Add the rice and dressing to a large bowl and mix well.

8. Add the tomatoes and mozzarella and mix again.

9. Finally, top with fresh basil leaves and serve immediately.

SERVING SUGGESTIONS:

For little ones, again I would suggest deconstructing and leaving off the dressing. Add any other colourful veg to the plate that you know they love. You could encourage trying mozzarella by popping on child-friendly sticks with the cherry tomatoes, too.

STORING AND FREEZING:

Leftover rice salad can be kept in an airtight container in the fridge for up to 3 days. Eating cold rice is safe, just be sure not to leave it sitting around at room temperature for too long before eating it or putting it in the fridge.

BACON MAC & CHEESE

| Serves: 4 | Prep time: 2 minutes | Cook time: 10 minutes | Calories: 415 without sides |

This cheat's mac and cheese is so easy to make with just a few simple ingredients and topped with crispy bacon.

INGREDIENTS

350g macaroni

spray oil

4 smoked bacon medallions

125g light spreadable cheese

100ml semi-skimmed milk

1 tbsp chopped fresh chives

SERVING SUGGESTIONS:

Let kids sort toppings for themselves, and encourage adding anything else they want on top, too! Serve with a side salad or crudités.

STORING:

Leftover mac and cheese can be stored in the fridge for up to 2 days and reheated in the microwave or on the hob. You may need to add some extra milk as the pasta will naturally dry out a little.

METHOD

1. Cook the macaroni in a saucepan of boiling water on the hob according to the package instructions.

2. In the meantime, add some spray oil to a frying pan and cook the bacon medallions for 3 minutes on either side. When cooked, cut into small pieces and set aside.

3. When the macaroni is cooked, drain it and return to the saucepan on the hob along with the spreadable cheese and milk.

4. Cook for 1 minute until the cheese has melted.

5. Divide between four bowls and top with the chopped bacon and chives.

CLUB SANDWICH

NF

| Serves: 4 | Prep time: 6 minutes | Cook time: none | Calories per sandwich: 500 |

You can't beat a simple club sandwich for a quick, easy and filling lunch at home.

INGREDIENTS

12 slices medium white bread

4 tbsp Lighter than Light mayonnaise

2 little gem lettuce

200g turkey ham

4 slices (100g) Edam cheese

200g wafer-thin chicken slices

4 tomatoes, sliced

SERVING SUGGESTIONS:

Serve immediately with a side salad for adults, and when making for younger children, you may want to deconstruct the sandwich and serve all the elements separated on the plate along with some crudités. Allow choice!

STORING:

This recipe is best eaten immediately after preparing.

METHOD

1. Toast the bread and spread the mayonnaise onto all the slices of toast.

2. Take one piece of toast and add some lettuce leaves, followed by some turkey ham and a slice of cheese.

3. Add another slice of toast on top of that and then add the chicken slices and tomato. Finish with a third slice of toast.

4. Cut the sandwiches into four quarters and repeat with the other ingredients to make four sandwiches in total.

KIMCHI CHEESE TOASTIE

| Makes: 4 | Prep time: 4 minutes | Cook time: 4 minutes | Calories: 350 for adult portion |

If you love Korean flavours, then you need to try this upgrade to the humble cheese toastie. Sweet, salty, spicy and sour all in one, it's the ultimate umami meal.

INGREDIENTS

For the adult toastie:

2 tsp chilli sauce
4 medium slices white bread
200g kimchi
50g grated Cheddar cheese
1 spring onion, chopped
handful of fresh coriander
spray oil

For the kids' toastie:

4 medium slices white bread
2 tsp butter
100g grated Cheddar cheese

> **STORING:**
> This recipe is best eaten immediately after cooking.

METHOD

Adults' version (makes two):

1. For the adult version, spread the chilli sauce onto two slices of bread.

2. Drain the kimchi well and divide this between the two slices of bread.

3. Top with the grated cheese, spring onion and a little coriander.

4. Place the remaining slices of bread on top to create two sandwiches.

5. Heat a little spray oil in a frying pan on the hob and cook the sandwiches on a low heat for 1.5-2 minutes on either side until golden brown.

6. Cut in two and serve immediately with a side salad.

Kids' version (makes two):

1. For the kids' version, butter the four slices of bread and add the grated cheese to two slices.

2. Place the remaining two slices of bread on top to create two sandwiches.

3. Heat a little spray oil in a frying pan on the hob and cook on a low heat for 1.5-2 minutes on either side until golden brown.

4. Cut in two and serve immediate with crudités.

RAINBOW VEGGIE WRAP

| Serves: 4 | Prep time: 5 minutes | Cook time: 4 minutes | Calories per portion: 360 |

Pack in several portions of veggies at lunch with this speedy hummus wrap.

INGREDIENTS

4 large tortilla wraps

200g hummus

2 little gem lettuce

2 medium carrots

200g cucumber

1 red pepper

½ red onion

handful of fresh parsley or coriander

SERVING SUGGESTIONS:

Serve immediately with a side salad for adults.

For children who are not keen on a vegetable-filled wrap, you could instead make a plain ham or cheese wrap and serve the vegetables on the side with their portion of hummus for dipping.

STORING:

This recipe is best eaten immediately after preparing.

METHOD

1. Add the tortilla wraps one at a time to a dry frying pan. Cook for 30 seconds on either side to warm them up.

2. Spread the hummus onto the wraps.

3. Prep the veggies. Remove the lettuce leaves from the stalk. Use a peeler to shave the carrots into thin strips. Cut the cucumber into thin half-moon slices. Cut the pepper into thin slices and cut the onion into thin rounds.

4. Add the veggies to the wraps along with some fresh parsley or coriander. Roll the wraps up as tightly as you can and cut in half.

NASI GORENG

| Serves: 4 | Prep time: 5 minutes | Cook time: 11 minutes | Calories: 335 per portion |

Use microwave rice to whip up this speedy Nasi Goreng for a delicious and filling lunch at home.

INGREDIENTS

1 tbsp oil

1 onion, diced

2 garlic cloves, crushed

2 spring onions, chopped

400g white cabbage, diced

2 packets of microwave rice or 500g cold cooked rice

2 tbsp soy sauce

2 tbsp fish sauce

4 medium eggs

To serve:

120g cucumber, sliced

2 tomatoes, sliced

chilli sauce

> **SERVING SUGGESTIONS:**
> For adults, drizzle on a little chilli sauce.

> **STORING:**
> This recipe is best eaten immediately after cooking.

METHOD

1. Add half the oil and the onions to a frying pan on the hob on a medium heat and cook for 2 minutes.

2. Add the garlic, the white of the spring onions and the cabbage and cook for another 2 minutes.

3. Add the rice (no need to microwave it first) along with 2 tablespoons of water and cook for 3 minutes, stirring constantly. (If you are cooking rice for this recipe, 190g of uncooked rice will give you approximately 500g of cooked rice.)

4. Add the soy sauce and fish sauce and mix well. Divide the rice between four plates or bowls.

5. Wipe the frying pan clean with some kitchen roll.

6. Add the remaining oil to the frying pan and heat on a medium heat. Crack in the eggs and fry for 3-4 minutes or longer if you prefer a firmer yolk.

7. Place the fried eggs on top of the rice and garnish with the greens of the spring onions.

8. Add the sliced cucumber and tomatoes to the side.

CHICKEN CAESAR PASTA SALAD

| Serves: 4 | Prep time: 10 minutes | Cook time: 10 minutes | Calories: 485 per portion |

All the delicious flavours of a Caesar salad bulked out with pasta for a filling, family-friendly lunch.

INGREDIENTS

For the salad:
1 small bread roll (70g)
½ tbsp oil
½ tsp garlic powder
salt and pepper
300g pasta
240g cooked chicken pieces
1 little gem lettuce, chopped

For the sauce:
100g fat-free Greek yogurt
50ml semi-skimmed milk
50g Lighter than Light mayonnaise
1 tsp Dijon mustard
½ tsp garlic powder
50g grated Parmesan cheese
salt and pepper

METHOD

1. Preheat the oven to 200°C Fan/220°C/Gas Mark 7.

2. Cut the bread into small pieces to make croutons and place on a baking tray.

3. Drizzle on the oil, add the garlic powder and a little salt and pepper and mix well.

4. Bake for 8–10 minutes until the croutons are crispy.

5. Meanwhile, cook the pasta according to the package instructions. When cooked, drain and rinse under cold water to cool it down.

6. Add all the sauce ingredients to a large bowl. Mix in the chicken pieces until they are fully coated in the sauce.

7. Add the drained pasta and lettuce and mix again.

8. Divide the mixture between four bowls to serve, with the croutons on top.

SERVING SUGGESTIONS:

If your children prefer food to be separated on the plate, portion out some pasta before you mix it with the chicken and sauce. You could leave out the lettuce and replace with some crudités.

STORING:

Store in an airtight container in the fridge for up to 2 days. Store croutons at room temperature (they will go soft if left in the salad).

MELTY MOZZARELLA BAGELS

| Serves: 4 | Prep time: 3 minutes | Cook time: 8 minutes | Calories: 250 per portion (without side salad or crudités) |

This Italian-style bagel is wrapped in foil and baked in the oven, where all the ingredients melt together.

INGREDIENTS

4 bagel thins

3 tbsp basil pesto

125g mozzarella ball

4 tomatoes

handful fresh basil

SERVING SUGGESTIONS:

Serve with a side salad or crudités. Introduce to your children as a different version of pizza, and for younger children, slice the bagel into more manageable pieces.

STORING:

This bagel is best eaten immediately after cooking.

METHOD

1. Preheat the oven to 200°C Fan/220°C/Gas Mark 7.

2. Open the bagel thins and add a little pesto to both sides of the bagel.

3. Cut the mozzarella and tomatoes into thin slices and add these to the bagel along with a few basil leaves.

4. Wrap the bagels individually in foil, place on a baking tray and bake for 8 minutes.

CRISPY TORTILLA PIZZAS

| Serves: 1 | Prep time: 5 minutes | Cook time: 4 minutes | Calories: 300 for Margherita, 350 for Pesto Veggie |

These Tortilla Pizzas are cooked under the grill for a speedy lunch at home, with two options for toppings depending on what you and the kids enjoy.

MARGHERITA INGREDIENTS

1 large tortilla wrap
2 tbsp tomato purée
¼ tsp garlic powder
¼ tsp dried oregano
1 tomato
40g mozzarella

To garnish:
salt and pepper
fresh basil leaves

PESTO VEGGIE INGREDIENTS

1 large tortilla wrap
2 tbsp basil pesto
5 cherry tomatoes
5 pitted black olives
½ yellow pepper

To garnish:
salt and pepper
fresh basil leaves

> ### SERVING SUGGESTIONS:
> Serve immediately with a side salad or crudités.

> ### STORING:
> This recipe is best eaten immediately after cooking.

METHOD

Margherita version

1. Prick the tortilla wrap with a fork in a few places.

2. Place under the grill for 2 minutes until it starts to brown but be careful not to burn it. Remove from the grill and turn the wrap over.

3. Mix the tomato purée, garlic powder and oregano together; spread on the uncooked side of the wrap.

4. Cut the tomato and mozzarella into thin slices and add these to the top.

5. Place the wrap back under the grill for another 2–3 minutes until the mozzarella has melted.

6. Season with a little salt and pepper and top with fresh basil leaves.

METHOD

Pesto Veggie version

1. Prick the tortilla wrap with a fork in a few places.

2. Place under the grill for 2 minutes until it starts to brown but be careful not to burn it.

3. Remove from the grill and turn the wrap over Spread the pesto over the uncooked side of the wrap.

4. Chop the tomatoes and olives in half, cut the pepper into thin slices and add to top the pesto.

5. Place the wrap back under the grill for another 2-3 minutes.

6. Season with a little salt and pepper and top with fresh basil leaves.

PROSCIUTTO EGG MUFFINS

| Serves: 4 | Prep time: 7 minutes | Cook time: 15 minutes | Calories: 230 per two muffins |

Mini-quiche without the pastry, these egg muffins are super tasty and great to batch make and keep in the fridge for another day.

INGREDIENTS

spray oil

8 slices prosciutto

100g cherry tomatoes

1 spring onion

50g grated Cheddar cheese

6 medium eggs

salt and pepper

SERVING SUGGESTIONS:

Serve immediately with a side salad or crudités. For younger children, chop the muffins into more manageable bite-sized pieces.

STORING:

Leftover muffins can be kept in an airtight container in the fridge for up to 3 days and either eaten cold or reheated in the microwave.

METHOD

1. Preheat the oven to 180°C Fan/200°C/Gas Mark 6.

2. Spray a muffin tray with spray oil. You can use a metal or silicone muffin tray, or separate silicone muffin cases.

3. Push one slice of prosciutto into eight of the muffin holes.

4. Chop the cherry tomatoes and spring onion into small, diced pieces and divide these amongst the eight muffin holes on top of the prosciutto. Sprinkle on the grated cheese.

5. Crack the eggs into a jug and whisk with a fork. Season with a little salt and pepper.

6. Pour the whisked eggs into the muffin holes.

7. Bake in the oven for 15–18 minutes until the eggs have set.

8. Leave to cool in the muffin tray for 5 minutes before removing.

GRAZING BOARD LUNCH

Grazing boards are my ultimate treat lunch. Portioning out all the ingredients means it's easy to keep a board healthy, whilst being filling at the same time.

INGREDIENTS

8 slices chorizo

4 slices Parma ham

120g Cheddar cheese, cut into four

4 mini Brie triangles or 120g Brie, cut into four

80g mini breadsticks

300g cherry tomatoes

200g cucumber, sliced

200g grapes

50g pitted black olives

1 large carrot, cut into sticks

1 yellow pepper, sliced

4 celery sticks, cut into sticks

METHOD

1. Add all the ingredients to a large board or divide between four plates.

2. Serve immediately.

3. Any cheeses or meats that your children don't enjoy can be swapped for others, of course – put new foods next to trusty ones, make the board as colourful as possible. Even use paper picnic plates you can recycle!

> ### STORING:
> This recipe is best eaten immediately after assembling.

WEEKDAY MEALS

Spaghetti Puttanesca
Chicken Shawarma Salad
Creamy Chipotle Prawn Pasta
Jerk Chicken & Sweetcorn Salsa
Sweet & Sticky Veggie Noodles
Fish Finger Sandwich
Blue Cheese & Crispy Onion Smash Burger
Dan Dan Noodles
Salt & Pepper Chicken Noodles
Bang Bang Salmon Bowl
Hoisin Chicken Wraps
One-Pot Chicken Bolognese
Vegetable Biryani with Raita
Lemon & Pea Rigatoni
Harissa Chicken Burgers
Seafood Linguine
Roasted Tomato & Basil Spaghetti
Tikka Masala Paneer Naan
Roasted Red Pepper Gnocchi
Honey Lamb Kofta
Lemon Chicken Orzo

SPAGHETTI PUTTANESCA

| Serves: 4 | Prep time: 4 minutes | Cook time: 17 minutes | Calories: 390 (not including any cheese or side salad) |

Upgrade your simple tomato pasta with just a few ingredients! You may be sceptical of using anchovies, especially for children, but they melt into the sauce and give a delicious salty flavour without being overwhelming, I promise! Try it and let me know what you think.

INGREDIENTS

½ tbsp oil

½ tbsp butter

1 onion, chopped

2 garlic cloves, crushed

6 anchovy fillets, chopped

20g capers

400g tin chopped tomatoes

40g pitted black olives, halved

350g spaghetti

To garnish:

fresh parsley and dried chilli flakes

SERVING SUGGESTIONS:

Serve the adults' portion with dried chilli flakes on top and the children's portion with a little grated cheese. You can also serve a salad on the side.

STORING:

Leftovers can be kept in an airtight container in the fridge for up to 2 days and reheated on the hob or in the microwave.

METHOD

1. Add the oil, butter and onion to a large frying pan or shallow casserole dish.

2. Cook for 3 minutes until the onions have softened.

3. Add the garlic and chopped anchovies and continue to cook for another 2 minutes.

4. Add the capers, tinned tomatoes and olives. Bring to the boil and simmer for 10 minutes.

5. Meanwhile, cook the spaghetti in a large saucepan according to the package instructions.

6. When the spaghetti is cooked, remove half a cup of the pasta water and add that to the tomato sauce.

7. Drain the spaghetti and mix it in with the sauce.

8. Add some chopped fresh parsley on top.

CHICKEN SHAWARMA SALAD

| Serves: 4 | Prep time: 10 mins, plus minimum 1 hour to marinate | Cook time: 15 minutes | Calories: 365 per portion (not incl. pitta bread) |

This salad is perfect for a light and fresh spring or summer meal. Add pitta bread or flatbreads for a more substantial dinner that the whole family will enjoy.

INGREDIENTS

For the chicken shawarma:

2 tbsp oil

juice of 1 lemon

1 tsp garlic powder

1 tsp smoked paprika

1 tsp ground cumin

1 tsp dried oregano

salt and pepper

600g skinless and boneless chicken thighs

For the salad:

100g mixed lettuce leaves

200g cucumber

150g cherry tomatoes

1 yellow pepper

½ red onion

For the sauce:

150g fat-free Greek yogurt

juice of ½ lemon

1 tsp garlic powder

salt and pepper

METHOD

1. Add the oil, lemon juice, garlic powder, paprika, cumin and oregano to a large bowl. Season with a little salt and pepper and mix well.

2. Cut the chicken thighs into thin strips and mix with the marinade.

3. Cover and leave in the fridge for a minimum of 1 hour. I usually make the marinade in the morning or the night before and then leave in the fridge.

4. When ready to cook, remove from the fridge and add the marinated chicken thighs to a large frying pan or shallow casserole dish.

5. Cook on a medium heat on the hob for 15 minutes until the chicken is starting to crisp up, turning every few minutes.

6. In the meantime, make the salad. Divide the lettuce between four bowls and chop the cucumber, cherry tomatoes, pepper and red onion, adding to the top of the lettuce.

7. Mix the ingredients together to make the sauce.

8. Serve the cooked chicken shawarma on top of the salad and drizzle on the sauce.

SERVING SUGGESTIONS:

For kids, separate the salad from the chicken and add strips of toasted pitta bread.

STORING:

The salad is best eaten straight away. Store leftover chicken and sauce in an airtight container in the fridge for up to 2 days. Leftover chicken can be frozen for up to 2 months and defrosted in the fridge overnight.

CREAMY CHIPOTLE PRAWN PASTA

| Serves: 4 | Prep time: 5 minutes | Cook time: 18 minutes | Calories: 500 per portion (without side salad or garlic bread) |

My children are not usually massive seafood fans, but they will happily eat this prawn pasta
cooked in a mildly spicy but creamy sauce.

INGREDIENTS

½ tbsp oil

1 onion, diced

2 garlic cloves, crushed

1 red pepper, chopped

1 yellow pepper, chopped

½ tbsp chipotle paste

400g tin chopped tomatoes

200ml water

200g frozen raw prawns

350g pasta

100g half-fat crème fraîche

40g grated Parmesan Cheese

SERVING SUGGESTIONS:

Serve the adults' portion with a side
salad and the kids' portion with some
garlic bread.

STORING:

Leftovers can be kept in an airtight
container in the fridge for up to
2 days and reheated on the hob or
in the microwave.

METHOD

1. Add the oil and onion to a large, shallow casserole
    dish on the hob and cook for 2–3 minutes.

2. Add the garlic, peppers and chipotle paste and
    cook for a further 2 minutes.

3. Add the tinned tomatoes and water and bring
    to the boil.

4. Reduce to a simmer and add the prawns.
    Cook for 8–10 minutes until the prawns are fully
    cooked through.

5. In the meantime, add the pasta to a saucepan of
    boiling water on the hob and cook according to
    the package instructions.

6. When the prawns are cooked, turn the heat
    off and add the crème fraîche and Parmesan.
    Mix well.

7. Drain the pasta and add to the prawns, stirring one
    last time.

JERK CHICKEN & SWEETCORN SALSA

| Serves: 4 | Prep time: 6 minutes | Cook time: 12 minutes | Calories: 375 without rice, 545 with rice |

Use a jar of jerk seasoning to transform a simple chicken breast into a tasty meal, along with a fresh and zesty sweetcorn salad. This recipe works really well on the BBQ too.

INGREDIENTS

For the chicken:

4 medium (650g) chicken breasts

2 tbsp oil

3 tsp jerk seasoning

salt and pepper

For the sweetcorn salsa:

120g cucumber

120g cherry tomatoes

1 red pepper

1 small avocado

½ red onion

150g tinned sweetcorn

handful of fresh coriander

1 tbsp olive oil

2 tsp honey

juice of 1 lime

salt and pepper

To serve:

2 packets long-grain microwave rice or 500g of cooked rice

METHOD

1. Place the chicken breasts between two pieces of cling film or foil and bash them with a rolling pin to about 1cm thick.

2. Mix the oil and jerk seasoning with a little salt and pepper and brush onto the chicken breasts.

3. Cook the chicken breasts on a grill pan on a medium heat on the hob for 5-6 minutes on either side. Check to ensure they are fully cooked inside.

4. Make the sweetcorn salsa by chopping the cucumber, cherry tomatoes, red pepper, avocado and red onion into small, bite-sized pieces.

5. Add to a large bowl with the sweetcorn. Finely chop the fresh coriander and add that too.

6. Mix the olive oil, honey and lime juice in a small bowl and season with salt and pepper.

7. Mix the dressing with the sweetcorn salsa.

8. Cook the microwave rice according to the package instructions. If you are cooking rice for this recipe, 190g of uncooked rice will give you approximately 500g of cooked rice.

9. Slice the jerk chicken into strips and serve on plates with the cooked rice and sweetcorn salsa.

SERVING SUGGESTIONS:

For children who may be unsure of the sweetcorn salsa, serve a very small portion alongside some veggies or crudités.

STORING:

Keep leftovers in an airtight container in the fridge for up to 2 days. The chicken can be reheated on the hob or in the microwave.

SWEET & STICKY VEGGIE NOODLES

| Serves: 4 | Prep time: 7 minutes | Cook time: 10 minutes | Calories: 530 per portion |

Ramen noodles get a bad rap for being unhealthy but by cutting down the seasoning and adding lots of veggies, they can make a really delicious family meal.

INGREDIENTS

For the noodles and veggies:

½ tbsp oil

1 onion, sliced

2 garlic cloves, crushed

1 large carrot, shaved into thin strips with a vegetable peeler

1 red pepper, thinly sliced

300g Chinese cabbage or white cabbage, thinly sliced

100g baby corn, cut in half lengthways

100g sugar snap peas

300g ramen noodles

For the sauce:

2 tbsp sweet chilli sauce

2 tbsp ketchup

2 tbsp soy sauce

2 tbsp honey

100ml water

To serve:

20g crispy dried onions

METHOD

1. Heat the oil in a wok on a medium heat on the hob. Add the onion and cook for 3 minutes.

2. Add the garlic, carrot shavings, red pepper, cabbage, baby corn and sugar snap peas and cook for another 3 minutes, stirring regularly.

3. Add the ramen noodles (without the packets of seasoning) to a saucepan of boiling water. (Most ramen noodles are dairy- and egg-free but check the ingredients of the ones that you buy to be sure.)

4. Cook according to the package instructions, usually about 4 minutes.

5. Take one of the seasoning packets from the ramen noodles and add to a small jug or mug with the sweet chilli sauce, ketchup, soy sauce, honey and water. Mix well. Pour over the vegetables and cook for 1 minute until the sauce starts to thicken.

7. Once the noodles are cooked, drain and add them to the wok with the vegetables and sauce. Mix well.

8. Divide between four plates or bowls and serve with crispy onions on top.

SERVING SUGGESTIONS:

For children who prefer their food separated, you can portion out their noodles before adding them to the wok. Serve alongside the veggies and sauce.

STORING:

Leftovers can be kept in an airtight container in the fridge for up to 2 days and reheated on the hob or in the microwave.

FISH FINGER SANDWICH

| Serves: 4 | Prep time: 10 minutes | Cook time: 18 minutes | Calories: 460 (not incl. side salad) |

Chunky homemade fish fingers make a brilliant and nutritious mid-week sandwich dinner.

INGREDIENTS

For the fish fingers:

500g (approx. 4 fillets) skinless and boneless white fish (cod, haddock, pollock, hake etc.)

40g plain flour

2 medium eggs

60g panko breadcrumbs

1 tsp lemon pepper (or ¼ tsp black pepper)

¼ tsp salt

1 tbsp oil

For the sauce:

5 tbsp Lighter than Light mayonnaise

2 tsp capers, chopped

juice of ½ lemon

To serve:

4 burger buns

1 little gem lettuce

handful of lettuce leaves

2 tomatoes, sliced

METHOD

1. Cut the fish into chunky rectangles. You should be able to make 12 fish fingers from 4 fillets.

2. Pour the flour onto a plate. Crack the eggs into a bowl and whisk gently with a fork. Add the panko breadcrumbs, lemon pepper and salt to another plate and mix well.

3. Coat each fish finger in the flour, dip in the egg and then roll in the panko mixture.

4. Heat the oil in a large frying pan on a low heat and cook the fish fingers for approximately 4 minutes on either side. Turn them on the remaining shorter sides and cook for another minute just so they are evenly browned. You will probably have to do this in two batches.

5. In the meantime, make the sauce by mixing together the mayonnaise, capers and lemon juice.

6. Toast the burger buns in the toaster or under the grill and layer with the sauce, lettuce leaves and sliced tomatoes.

7. Finally, add the fish fingers and serve immediately with a side salad or crudités.

SERVING SUGGESTIONS:

For younger children it may be easier to serve the fish fingers chopped into more manageable bite-sized pieces and the burger buns cut into slices.

STORING:

These fish fingers are best eaten immediately after cooking. However, they can be prepped up to 6 hours ahead and kept in the fridge until ready to cook.

BLUE CHEESE & CRISPY ONION SMASH BURGER

| Serves: 4 | Prep time: 4 minutes | Cook time: 8 minutes | Calories: 435 per portion (without side salad) |

Smash burgers are my new favourite way to make beef burgers at home. The burgers are flattened down so that they cook quickly and on a high heat, so they get that lovely crisp coating on the outside.

INGREDIENTS

500g 5% fat beef mince
salt and pepper
½ tbsp oil
60g Saint Agur Blue Crème
40g crispy onions
4 brioche buns, halved
handful of lettuce leaves

> ### STORING:
> These burgers are best eaten immediately after cooking.

METHOD

1. Add the mince to a large bowl and season with a little salt and pepper. Mix well.

2. Shape the seasoned mince into 4 burgers.

3. Heat the oil in a frying pan or grill pan on a medium-high heat on the hob.

4. Add the burgers and flatten them down with a spatula until they are about 1cm thick.

5. Cook for 3-4 minutes on either side. Don't move the burgers in the pan other than when you are flipping them.

6. Toast the brioche buns.

7. Add lettuce to the bottom of each of the buns, followed by the burger, some Saint Agur Blue Crème and crispy onions.

8. If the kids are not keen on blue cheese, you can swap it for a slice of Cheddar cheese instead. Add it to the top of the burger after you have flipped it in the pan and allow to melt as the burger cooks.

9. Serve immediately with a side salad or crudités.

DAN DAN NOODLES

| Serves: 4 | Prep time: 4 minutes | Cook time: 14 minutes | Calories: 460 per portion |

This traditional Chinese dish is sweet and salty with a hint of spice for the adults. A great one to break up the monotony of cooking the same recipes every week.

INGREDIENTS

For the pork and noodles:

200g rice noodles

½ tbsp oil

500g 5% pork mince

2 garlic cloves, crushed

1cm piece of ginger, peeled and chopped

½ tsp Szechuan peppercorns, crushed

2 pak choi, stalks removed and sliced in half

2 spring onions, chopped

For the sauce:

300ml chicken stock

50g crunchy peanut butter

1 tbsp soy sauce

1 tbsp hoisin sauce

To serve:

chilli sauce

METHOD

1. Cook the noodles in a saucepan on the hob according to the package instructions. When cooked, drain and rinse under cold water.

2. Add the oil and pork mince to a wok on the hob on a medium heat and cook for 6-7 minutes.

3. Add the garlic, ginger and Szechuan peppercorns and cook for 1 minute.

4. Add the pak choi and the whites of the spring onions and cook for a further 2 minutes.

5. Mix the sauce ingredients in a small jug or mug and add to the wok. Cook for 1 minute until the sauce starts to thicken.

6. Turn off the heat and add the drained noodles.

7. Mix well and top with the green of the spring onions.

SERVING SUGGESTIONS:

Serve the adults' portion with a drizzle of chilli sauce on top. If you can't find Szechuan peppercorns, substitute with ⅛ tsp black pepper. For children who may prefer this separated, you can portion off their noodles before adding them to the wok and serve alongside the pork and vegetables.

STORING:

Leftovers can be kept in an airtight container in the fridge for up to 2 days and reheated on the hob or in the microwave.

SALT & PEPPER CHICKEN NOODLES

| Serves: 4 | Prep time: 10 minutes | Cook time: 18 minutes | Calories: 530 per portion |

Salt and Pepper Chicken is one of my family's takeaway favourites, but it's easy to make your own at home and turn it into a complete meal with noodles and vegetables too.

INGREDIENTS

For the chicken:

2 large (450g) chicken breasts

50g cornflour

2 tsp Chinese five spice

2 tsp garlic powder

1 tsp smoked paprika

¼ tsp salt

¼ tsp pepper

2 tbsp oil

For the noodles:

250g medium egg noodles

1 onion, sliced

2 garlic cloves, sliced

1 red pepper, sliced

1 yellow pepper, sliced

3 spring onions, chopped

For the sauce:

1 tbsp soy sauce

1 tbsp honey

1 tbsp ketchup

1 tbsp rice wine vinegar

50ml water

METHOD

1. Cut the chicken breast into thin strips.

2. On a large plate, mix the cornflour, Chinese five spice, garlic powder, smoked paprika, salt and pepper. Add the chicken to the plate and coat all the strips fully in the cornflour mixture.

4. Heat the oil in a wok or large frying pan. Add the chicken and cook on a high heat for 8 minutes until cooked through and crispy on the outside. Set the chicken aside and cover with foil to keep warm.

5. Cook the noodles in a saucepan on the hob according to the package instructions.

6. Add the onion, garlic, red and yellow peppers and white of the spring onions to the wok and cook for 5 minutes.

7. Mix together the soy sauce, honey, ketchup, rice wine vinegar and water in a small jug or cup. Pour this over the vegetables in the wok and cook for 1 minute until the sauce starts to thicken. Drain the noodles and add these to the wok, mixing well so that they absorb the sauce. Divide the noodles and vegetables between four plates or bowls and add the cooked chicken strips on top.

8. Garnish with the green of the spring onions.

SERVING SUGGESTIONS:

If your children prefer their food separated, portion out their noodles before you add them to the wok. Serve the noodles plain with the veggies and chicken on the side.

STORING:

Leftovers can be kept in an airtight container in the fridge for up to 2 days and reheated on the hob or in the microwave.

BANG BANG SALMON BOWL

GF   DF   NF

| Serves: 4 | Prep time: 15 minutes | Cook time: 7 minutes | Calories per portion: 565 |

With some simple seasoning you can transfer salmon fillets into tasty little fish bites, served up with rice and salad plus a spicy mayonnaise sauce.

INGREDIENTS

For the salmon:

4 salmon fillets, skin removed (500g)

1 tbsp oil

½ tsp garlic powder

½ tsp onion powder

½ tsp dried oregano

½ tsp lemon pepper (or ¼ tsp black pepper)

pinch of salt

For the rice and salad:

2 packets microwave rice or 500g cooked rice

2 carrots

300g cucumber

4 radishes

1 yellow pepper

2 spring onions

For the sauce:

4 tbsp Lighter than Light mayonnaise

2 tsp Sriracha or other chilli sauce

juice of ½ lime

salt and pepper

METHOD

1. Cut the salmon into bite-sized pieces.

2. Mix the oil, garlic powder, onion powder, oregano, lemon pepper and salt in a bowl. Add the salmon and toss so it is fully coated in the oil and spices.

3. Transfer the salmon to a frying pan and fry on a medium heat for 7-8 minutes, turning a few times, until cooked on the inside and crispy on the outside.

4. In the meantime, cook the microwave rice according to the package instructions and divide between four bowls. If you are cooking rice, 190g of uncooked rice will give you approximately 500g of cooked rice. Add the salmon pieces when they are cooked.

5. Use a vegetable peeler to create thin strips from the carrots and cucumber. Slice the radishes thinly. Slice the pepper into thin strips and chop the spring onions thinly. Add all the vegetables to the bowls.

6. To make the sauce, mix together the mayonnaise, Sriracha, lime juice and a little salt and pepper. Drizzle over the top of the salmon and vegetables.

SERVING SUGGESTIONS:

You don't need to change much for children here. If you think they'll find the sauce a bit spicy, then you can leave it out of their portion.

STORING:

The salad and rice should be eaten immediately. Store leftover salmon and sauce in an airtight container in the fridge for up to 2 days, or freeze for up to 2 months. Defrost overnight in the fridge.

HOISIN CHICKEN WRAPS

| Serves: 4 | Prep time: 8 minutes | Cook time: 19 minutes | Calories: 460 per portion |

These chicken wraps are a brilliant serve-yourself family meal. Let the kids choose their toppings and help themselves at the table for a more relaxed dinner time.

INGREDIENTS

For the chicken:

3 chicken breasts (500g)

150g hoisin sauce

2 tbsp honey

1 tsp sesame seeds

For the salad and wraps:

230g cucumber

1 large carrot

2 spring onions

2 little gem lettuce

8 mini tortilla wraps

To serve:

handful of fresh coriander

1 tbsp hoisin sauce

SERVING SUGGESTIONS:

Let everyone make their own wraps drizzled with the extra hoisin sauce on top.

STORING:

The salad is best eaten immediately, however any leftover chicken can be stored in an airtight container in the fridge for up to 2 days. Leftover chicken can be frozen for up to 2 months and defrosted in the fridge overnight.

METHOD

1. Add the whole chicken breasts to a saucepan of boiling water and poach on a low simmer for 17 minutes.

2. Whilst the chicken is cooking, prep the vegetables. Cut the cucumber and carrot into thin strips. You can also use a julienne peeler for this if you have one. Chop the spring onions into thin rounds. Wash the lettuce leaves.

3. When the chicken is cooked, drain and remove from the saucepan and shred with two forks on a chopping board.

4. Add the shredded chicken back into the saucepan with the hoisin sauce and honey.

5. Cook for 2 minutes to heat the sauce and then add the sesame seeds.

6. Add the chicken to a bowl and place on the table with the vegetables, mini wraps and coriander.

7. Mix the extra hoisin sauce with a little water to thin it down.

ONE-POT CHICKEN BOLOGNESE

| Serves: 4 | Prep time: 5 minutes | Cook time: 35 minutes | Calories: 585 (not incl. side salad or vegetables) |

For a lighter take on Bolognese, try my version using chicken mince instead. Everything is cooked together in one pot, including the pasta. Perfect for an easy dinner mid-week.

INGREDIENTS

½ tbsp oil

4 (approx. 130g) lean smoked bacon medallions, chopped

1 onion, diced

2 garlic cloves, crushed

2 carrots, finely diced

1 celery stick, diced

1 red pepper, chopped

500g 5% fat chicken mince

400g tin chopped tomatoes

1 litre chicken stock

1 tsp dried oregano

2 tbsp ketchup

300g pasta

50g grated Parmesan cheese

STORING:

Leftovers can be kept in an airtight container in the fridge for up to 2 days and reheated on the hob or in the microwave.

METHOD

1. Add the oil, bacon and onion to a large shallow casserole dish and cook on the hob for 3 minutes.

2. Add the garlic, carrots, celery and pepper and cook for another 2 minutes.

3. Add the chicken mince and cook until it has all browned.

4. Add the chopped tomatoes, chicken stock, oregano, ketchup and pasta.

5. Bring to the boil, reduce to a simmer and cook for 18–20 minutes, stirring a few times.

6. Once the pasta and veggies are fully cooked and the stock has nearly all absorbed, remove from the heat and stir in the grated Parmesan.

7. Serve with cooked green vegetables or a side salad.

VEGETABLE BIRYANI WITH RAITA

| Serves: 4 | Prep time: 10 minutes | Cook time: 23 minutes | Calories: 360 per portion |

Biryani is a great meal to make for children who don't like foods with a lot of sauce.
It's still bursting with Indian flavours and is all made in one pot.

INGREDIENTS

For the biryani:
250g basmati rice
½ tbsp oil
1 onion, diced
2 garlic cloves, crushed
1cm piece of ginger, peeled and chopped
3 tbsp mild curry paste
1 tbsp tomato purée
250g cauliflower, cut into small florets
150g fresh green beans
1 carrot, very finely diced
800ml vegetable stock (use gluten free stock)

For the raita:
150g fat-free yogurt
50g cucumber, finely chopped
1 tsp mint sauce
½ tsp garlic powder
¼ tsp garam masala
salt and pepper

To serve:
chopped fresh coriander

> **STORING:**
> Leftover biryani can be kept in an airtight container in the fridge for up to 2 days. It can be frozen for up to 2 months and defrosted in the fridge overnight.

METHOD

1. Soak the rice in a large saucepan or bowl for about 10 minutes, draining the water a couple of times and rinsing it a final time through a sieve.

2. Add the oil and onion to a large frying pan or shallow casserole dish on the hob and cook on low for 4 minutes.

3. Add the garlic and ginger and cook for another 1 minute. Then add the curry paste and tomato purée and mix well.

4. Add the soaked rice, cauliflower, green beans, carrot and vegetable stock. Bring to the boil, cover with a lid or a tight layer of foil and simmer on low for 12 minutes.

5. Turn the heat off but leave the lid/foil on for another 5 minutes. Don't be tempted to take it off yet as the rice will continue to cook.

6. In the meantime, make the raita by mixing together the yogurt, cucumber, mint sauce, garlic powder and garam masala. Season with a little salt and pepper.

7. After 5 minutes, remove the lid from the biryani and divide between four plates or bowls.

8. Serve the raita on top or on the side and garnish with a little fresh coriander.

LEMON & PEA RIGATONI

| Serves: 4 | Prep time: 1 minute | Cook time: 14 minutes | Calories: 485 per portion |

This creamy pasta dish is so quick and easy to make, and all cooked in one pan
for minimal washing up!

INGREDIENTS

350g rigatoni

150g frozen peas

165g light cream cheese

150ml semi-skimmed milk

zest and juice of 1 lemon

½ tsp garlic powder

70g grated Parmesan Cheese

To serve:

fresh basil leaves

SERVING SUGGESTIONS:

Serve the adults' portion with a side
salad and the kids' portion with some
garlic bread or crudités.

STORING:

Leftovers can be kept in an airtight
container in the fridge for up to
2 days and reheated on the hob or
in the microwave. You may need to
add a splash of milk if the pasta has
dried up a little.

METHOD

1. Cook the pasta in a large saucepan on the hob
   according to the package instructions.

2. Add the frozen peas to the pasta for the last
   3 minutes of cooking.

3. When the pasta and peas are cooked, drain and
   set aside.

4. In the same saucepan, add the cream cheese, milk,
   lemon zest and juice and the garlic powder.

5. Cook for 1-2 minutes until the cream cheese has
   completely melted.

6. Add the pasta and frozen peas, along with the
   grated Parmesan and mix well.

7. Divide between four plates or bowls and add the
   fresh basil leaves on top.

HARISSA CHICKEN BURGERS

| Serves: 4 | Prep time: 7 minutes | Cook time: 12 minutes | Calories: 365 per portion (not incl. side salad or crudités) |

Harissa is a brilliant store cupboard staple to liven up plain chicken. Served up with a griddled red pepper and zesty feta sauce, which transforms this chicken burger into a really flavoursome meal.

INGREDIENTS

For the burgers:

2 large (450g) chicken breasts

2 tbsp harissa paste

1 tbsp oil

1 red pepper

4 burger buns, halved

For the sauce:

100g fat-free Greek yogurt

juice of ½ lemon

¼ tsp garlic powder

salt and pepper

50g feta

STORING:

Leftover chicken and peppers can be kept in the fridge for up to 2 days and reheated in the microwave or on the hob. Leftover chicken can also be frozen for up to 2 months and defrosted at room temperature.

METHOD

1. Place the chicken breasts between two pieces of cling film or parchment paper and bash with a rolling pin to flatten them out. Try to make the chicken completely even in thickness.

2. Cut the chicken breasts in half to make four fillets.

3. Put the harissa paste and oil in a bowl and mix well, then coat the chicken in this paste on both sides.

4. Cut the red pepper into four pieces.

5. Put the coated chicken breasts and red pepper in a grill pan. I have a large grill pan that will fit everything, but if you are using a smaller one then you may have to do this in two batches.

6. Cook for 5-6 minutes on either side until the chicken is fully cooked through and the peppers have blackened.

7. Make the sauce by mixing together the yogurt, lemon juice, garlic powder and salt and pepper in a bowl. Add the feta and mash it into the sauce with a fork.

8. Toast the burger buns and add a little sauce to the bottom bun, followed by a piece of chicken and red pepper.

SEAFOOD LINGUINE

| Serves: 4 | Prep time: 3 minutes | Cook time: 15 minutes | Calories: 440 per portion (not including sides) |

Simple pasta dishes are always the best, and this garlic and chilli seafood linguine
is one of my favourites for a quick and easy mid-week meal.

INGREDIENTS

250g mixed frozen seafood
(prawns, mussels, squid, etc.)

350g linguine

½ tbsp butter

2 garlic cloves, crushed

¼ tsp chilli flakes

200g cherry tomatoes, halved

juice of 1 lemon

100g fresh baby spinach

salt and pepper

To serve:

50g grated Parmesan cheese

1 red chilli, sliced

> ### SERVING SUGGESTIONS:
> Serve the adults' portion with some
> sliced chillies on top and a side salad
> and the kids' portion with garlic bread
> or crudités.

> ### STORING:
> Leftovers can be kept in an airtight
> container in the fridge for up to
> 2 days and reheated on the hob or
> in the microwave.

METHOD

1. Add the frozen seafood to a large frying pan or
   shallow casserole dish. Cover with boiling water
   and cook on the hob for 3 minutes. Drain the
   seafood and leave it in the pan.

2. Cook the linguine in a saucepan according to the
   package instructions.

3. To the seafood, add the butter, garlic, chilli flakes
   and cherry tomatoes. Cook for 4 minutes.

4. Add the lemon juice, spinach and a little salt and
   pepper and cook for a further 2 minutes.

5. Remove half a cup of the water that the linguine is
   cooking in and set aside.

6. Drain the linguine and add it to the seafood and
   mix well.

7. Add a little of the reserved pasta water and
   mix again.

8. Divide between four bowls or plates and add the
   grated Parmesan on top.

ROASTED TOMATO & BASIL SPAGHETTI

| Serves: 4 | Prep time: 2 minutes | Cook time: 17 minutes | Calories: 445 (not incl. sides) |

Roast cherry tomatoes to create a really easy and tasty pasta sauce. It's light and summery rather than being heavy, like many tomato-based pastas.

INGREDIENTS

500g cherry tomatoes

3 garlic cloves

2 tbsp olive oil

½ tsp dried oregano

salt and pepper

350g spaghetti

50g grated Parmesan cheese

handful fresh basil

SERVING SUGGESTIONS:

Serve the adults' portion with a side salad and the kids' portion with some garlic bread or crudités.

STORING:

Leftovers can be kept in an airtight container in the fridge for up to 2 days and reheated on the hob or in the microwave.

METHOD

1. Preheat the oven to 200°C Fan/220°C/Gas Mark 7.

2. Add the cherry tomatoes whole to a baking dish. Peel the garlic and add that whole, along with the olive oil, oregano and a little salt and pepper.

3. Mix well and roast in the oven for 15 minutes.

4. In the meantime, cook the spaghetti on the hob according to the package instructions.

5. When the spaghetti is almost cooked, remove half a cup of the pasta water and set aside.

6. Remove the dish from the oven and use a fork to mash the tomatoes and garlic.

7. Drain the spaghetti and add that to the baking dish and mix well.

8. Add a little of the reserved pasta water along with the Parmesan and mix again.

9. Divide between four plates or bowls.

10. Roughly tear the basil leaves and serve on top of the spaghetti.

TIKKA MASALA PANEER NAAN

| Serves: 4 | Prep time: 4 minutes | Cook time: 17 minutes | Calories: 575 per portion |

Paneer makes a great alternative to meat for a speedy mid-week curry. I serve mine on top of a warmed naan, but you could also swap it for rice instead.

INGREDIENTS

½ tbsp oil

1 onion, diced

2 garlic cloves, crushed

1cm piece of ginger, peeled and chopped

1 tbsp mild curry powder

1 tsp garam masala

400g tin chopped tomatoes

1 tbsp mango chutney

200ml vegetable stock

100g fresh green beans

200g paneer

100g fat-free yogurt

4 large naan (make your own, page 145)

To serve:

chopped fresh coriander

METHOD

1. Add the oil and onion to a saucepan on the hob and cook for 3 minutes.

2. Add the garlic and ginger and cook for another 1 minute.

3. Add the curry powder and garam masala and cook for about 30 seconds, stirring constantly.

4. Add the chopped tomatoes, mango chutney, vegetable stock and green beans.

5. Bring to the boil and simmer on low for 5 minutes.

6. Chop the paneer into approximately 2cm cubes and add to the pan.

7. Cook for a further 5 minutes until the paneer has warmed through.

8. In the meantime, preheat the oven to 180°C Fan/200°C/Gas Mark 6 and cook the naan according to the package instructions.

9. Serve the tikka masala paneer on top of the warmed naan and sprinkle with chopped coriander.

> **SERVING SUGGESTIONS:**
>
> For younger children, you could serve the curry in a small bowl and cut the naan into strips for dipping instead.

> **STORING:**
>
> Leftover curry can be kept in an airtight container in the fridge for up to 2 days and reheated in the microwave or on the hob. It can be frozen for up to 2 months and defrosted at room temperature.

ROASTED RED PEPPER GNOCCHI

| Serves: 4 | Prep time: 3 minutes | Cook time: 17 minutes | Calories: 325 (not incl. sides) |

Use a jar of roasted peppers to make an easy and delicious sauce for gnocchi.
Packed with flavour, and so quick too.

INGREDIENTS

360g drained jar of roasted red peppers
2 garlic cloves, peeled but left whole
½ tsp dried oregano
salt and pepper
400g tin chopped tomatoes
500g gnocchi
125g mozzarella ball
handful of fresh basil leaves

SERVING SUGGESTIONS:

Serve the adults' portion with a side salad and the kids' portion with some garlic bread.

STORING:

Leftovers can be kept in an airtight container in the fridge for up to 2 days and reheated on the hob or in the microwave.

METHOD

1. Add the roasted red peppers, garlic, oregano and a little salt and pepper to a blender and blitz until smooth.

2. Add the chopped tomatoes and blitz again.

3. Pour this mixture into a large frying pan or shallow casserole dish on the hob and simmer on low for 5 minutes.

4. Add the gnocchi, mix well and continue to simmer on low for another 7–8 minutes until the gnocchi is cooked through.

5. Tear the mozzarella ball into small pieces and lay these on top of the gnocchi.

6. Pop the dish under the grill for 3–4 minutes until the cheese has melted.

7. Top with fresh basil leaves.

HONEY LAMB KOFTA

| Serves: 4 | Prep time: 10 minutes | Cook time: 14 minutes | Calories: 535 (incl. pitta and salad) |

Lamb can be a particularly strong flavour for kids, but this kofta recipe contains honey, giving them a subtle sweetness, and it's packed with aromatic fresh herbs too.

INGREDIENTS

For the kofta:

500g 20% fat lamb mince
½ small red onion, finely diced
1 garlic clove, crushed
1 tbsp chopped fresh parsley
1 tbsp chopped fresh mint
1 tbsp honey
1 tsp ground cumin
salt and pepper

For the sauce:

100g cucumber
200g fat-free Greek yogurt
1 tsp chopped fresh mint
salt and pepper

To serve:

4 pitta bread
2 little gem lettuce
4 tomatoes, sliced
50g cucumber, sliced

STORING:

The salad is best eaten immediately, however any leftover kofta and sauce can be stored in an airtight container in the fridge for up to 2 days. Leftover kofta and sauce can be frozen for up to 2 months and defrosted in the fridge overnight.

METHOD

1. Add the lamb mince, red onion, garlic, parsley, mint, honey and cumin to a large bowl. Season with a little salt and pepper and mix really well until all the ingredients are well combined.

2. Form the lamb mixture into oval meatball shapes. You should be able to make 16 kofta.

3. Line a grill pan with foil. Thread the kofta onto three large or six shorter metal skewers and place these on the lined grill pan.

4. Cook under a hot grill for 7 minutes, turn and cook on the other side for another 7 minutes.

5. The kofta should be browned and crispy on the outside. Check the inside to ensure that they are fully cooked.

6. In the meantime, make the sauce by finely dicing the cucumber. Add it to a bowl with the yogurt, chopped mint and season with a little salt and pepper. Mix well.

7. Toast the pitta bread and serve family style at the table with the kofta and salad, letting everyone help themselves.

LEMON CHICKEN ORZO

| Serves: 4 | Prep time: 4 minutes | Cook time: 17 minutes | Calories: 525 per portion |

Poaching chicken is a great way to make it soft and easier to eat for children who may not usually like the texture. Served on top of a fresh and zesty lemon orzo, it makes a really tasty mid-week meal.

INGREDIENTS

2 chicken breasts (300g)

½ tbsp oil

1 onion, chopped

2 garlic cloves, crushed

400g orzo

½ tsp dried oregano

1 litre chicken stock

zest and juice of 1 lemon

100g fresh baby spinach

50g grated Parmesan cheese

To garnish:
chopped fresh chives

SERVING SUGGESTIONS:

For adults, serve with a side salad and for kids serve with garlic bread or crudités.

STORING:

Leftovers can be kept in an airtight container in the fridge for up to 2 days and reheated on the hob or in the microwave.

METHOD

1. Add the whole chicken breasts to a saucepan of boiling water and poach on a low simmer for 17 minutes.

2. In the meantime, add the oil, onion and garlic to a large frying pan or shallow casserole dish and cook for 3 minutes.

3. Add the orzo, oregano, chicken stock and lemon zest and juice.

4. Bring to the boil, reduce to a simmer and cook for 10 minutes, checking that the orzo is fully cooked.

5. Turn off the heat and add the baby spinach and Parmesan, mixing well.

6. When the chicken is cooked, remove from the saucepan and shred with two forks.

7. Divide the orzo between four bowls, add the shredded chicken to the top and garnish with chopped chives.

WEEKEND MEALS

Chicken Meatball Sub
Crispy Turkey Burger
Loaded Greek Potato Wedges with Crispy Halloumi
Salmon Risotto
Creamy Garlic & Herb Chicken with Parmesan Potatoes
Sesame-crusted Cod Tacos
Cauliflower Bolognese
Chicken & Spinach Lasagne
Crispy Korean Beef
Mediterranean Sausage Traybake
Buffalo & BBQ Chicken Wings with Blue Cheese Dip
Veggie Enchilada Lasagne
Tandoori Chicken Drumsticks
Baked Chorizo Rice

CHICKEN MEATBALL SUB

| Serves: 4 | Prep time: 12 minutes | Cook time: 20 minutes | Calories: 520 per portion (not incl. side salad or vegetables) |

Herby homemade chicken meatballs in a rich tomato sauce, all served up in a warm bread roll: the perfect Saturday night meal at home.

INGREDIENTS

For the meatballs:

400g 5% fat chicken mince

25g dried breadcrumbs

40g finely grated Parmesan cheese

1 medium egg

1 tsp onion powder

1 tsp garlic powder

1 tsp dried oregano

salt and pepper

spray oil

For the sauce:

2 x 400g tins chopped tomatoes

½ tsp dried oregano

salt and pepper

To serve:

4 small part-baked rolls (75g each)

75g grated mozzarella

fresh basil

STORING:

Leftover meatballs and sauce can be kept in an airtight container in the fridge for up to 2 days. They can be frozen for up to 2 months and defrosted in the fridge overnight.

METHOD

1. Add the chicken mince to a large bowl with the breadcrumbs, grated Parmesan and egg and mix well. (If you can't find chicken mince, turkey mince will work well too. Or you can blitz chicken breasts in a food processor to make your own.)

2. Add the onion powder, garlic powder and oregano and season with a little salt and pepper. Mix again.

3. Form the mixture in 20 evenly sized meatballs.

4. Add some spray oil to a large saucepan on the hob.

5. Add the meatballs and fry for 5 minutes, turning the meatballs so that they are evenly cooked on all sides.

6. Add the tinned tomatoes, oregano and little salt and pepper to the pan with the meatballs.

7. Continue to cook for another 10-12 minutes, turning the meatballs once. Ensure they are fully cooked on the inside.

8. In the meantime, preheat the oven and then cook the part-baked rolls according to the package instructions.

9. When baked, remove the bread rolls from the oven, cut with a knife to open and add the meatballs and sauce.

10. Sprinkle the grated mozzarella on top and pop under the grill for 1-2 minutes to melt the cheese.

11. Serve immediately with fresh basil leaves to garnish and with a side salad or portion of cooked vegetables.

CRISPY TURKEY BURGER

| Serves: 4 | Prep time: 7 minutes | Cook time: 25 minutes | Calories: 500 (incl. bun and toppings) |

A lot of people find turkey a bit bland and boring. But the key to this recipe is the cheese and onion crisp coating, which adds lots of flavour.

INGREDIENTS

4 (400g) turkey breast steaks

2 medium eggs

50g dried breadcrumbs

50g cheese and onion crisps

salt and pepper

spray oil

4 brioche buns

To serve:

1 little gem lettuce

2 tomatoes, sliced

4 tbsp Lighter than Light mayonnaise

SERVING SUGGESTIONS:

For younger children, you may want to cut the cooked turkey burger into strips and serve alongside the brioche and salad so that it is easier for them to eat.

STORING:

These turkey burgers are best eaten immediately after cooking. They will, however, keep in the fridge for up to 2 days and can be reheated in the oven.

METHOD

1. Preheat the oven to 180°C Fan/200°C/Gas Mark 6 and line a baking tray with parchment paper.

2. Crack the eggs into a bowl and whisk with a fork.

3. Add the breadcrumbs to another bowl.

4. Crush the crisps in their packet and then add to the breadcrumbs along with a little salt and pepper and mix well.

5. Take one of the turkey steaks, dip it in the egg and then coat in the crisp and breadcrumb mixture on both sides.

6. Place on the baking tray and repeat with the remaining turkey steaks. Spray the top with a little spray oil.

7. Bake in the oven for 25 minutes.

8. Serve each turkey steak in a brioche bun topped with lettuce, slices of tomato and mayonnaise.

LOADED GREEK POTATO WEDGES WITH CRISPY HALLOUMI

| Serves: 4 | Prep time: 15 minutes | Cook time: 45 minutes | Calories per portion: 585 |

I absolutely love halloumi, but I've struggled to get the kids to eat it – until I made this recipe. By coating it in panko breadcrumbs it creates crispy little nuggets, which are so tasty served on top of Greek potato wedges and salad.

INGREDIENTS

For the potatoes:

1.25kg Maris Piper potatoes

2 tbsp oil

juice of ½ lemon

1 tsp garlic powder

1 tsp smoked paprika

1 tsp dried oregano

salt and pepper

For the halloumi:

225g halloumi

1 medium egg

40g panko breadcrumbs

½ tsp garlic powder

½ tsp smoked paprika

spray oil

For sauce and salad ingredients, see overleaf.

METHOD

1. Preheat the oven to 200°C Fan/220°C/Gas Mark 7 and line a large baking tray with parchment paper.

2. Leaving the skins on, cut the potatoes into wedges and add them to a large bowl filled with water.

3. Leave the potatoes to soak for 10 minutes.

4. In the meantime, mix the oil, lemon juice, garlic powder, smoked paprika, oregano and a little salt and pepper together in a small bowl.

5. Drain the potatoes and add them to the lined baking tray. Pour the sauce over the wedges and mix well.

6. Bake in the oven for 45 minutes until cooked through and crispy.

7. To make the crispy halloumi, cut the block of halloumi into bite-sized pieces of approximately 2cm.

8. Crack the egg into a bowl and whisk with a fork.

9. Add the panko breadcrumbs, garlic powder and smoked paprika to another bowl and mix well.

10. Take half the halloumi pieces and add them to the bowl with the egg. Mix to ensure they are coated in the egg on all sides.

11. Transfer to the bowl with the panko breadcrumbs and mix, again ensuring they are fully coated.

12. Place on another baking tray and repeat the process with the rest of the halloumi pieces.

For the sauce:
100g fat-free Greek yogurt
1 tsp mint sauce
juice of ½ lemon
salt and pepper

For the salad:
200g cherry tomatoes
200g cucumber
50g pitted black olives
½ red onion
handful of fresh parsley

SERVING SUGGESTIONS:

For children, serve all the items separated on a plate with the sauce in a small dish for dipping.

STORING:

This recipe is best eaten immediately after cooking. Leftover potatoes and halloumi can be kept in the fridge for up to 2 days, but they will lose their crunch.

---

13. Spray the halloumi with some spray oil and bake in the oven for 18–20 minutes until golden brown.

14. To make the sauce, mix together the yogurt, mint sauce, lemon juice and a little salt and pepper together in a small bowl.

15. Chop the salad ingredients into small pieces.

16. When the wedges and halloumi pieces are cooked, remove from the oven.

17. Divide the potato wedges between four plates. Top with the salad ingredients and the halloumi pieces and drizzle on the sauce.

SALMON RISOTTO

| Serves: 4 | Prep time: 5 minutes | Cook time: 35 minutes | Calories: 450 per portion (not incl. side salad) |

This oven-baked risotto is so much easier than standing over the hob. It's creamy and cheesy and a great way to introduce salmon to fussy eaters.

INGREDIENTS

For the risotto:

½ tbsp oil

1 onion, diced

1 garlic clove, crushed

1 leek, chopped

300g risotto rice

1 litre hot vegetable stock

100g frozen peas

40g grated Parmesan cheese

For the salmon:

3 frozen salmon fillets (350g)

1 tbsp butter

1 garlic clove, crushed

salt and pepper

SERVING SUGGESTIONS:

If your children do not like fish, start by serving the salmon on the side instead of mixing their portion in with the risotto.

STORING:

This risotto can be kept in an airtight container in the fridge for up to 2 days. It can be frozen for up to 2 months and defrosted in the fridge overnight.

METHOD

1. Preheat the oven to 180°C Fan/200°C/Gas Mark 6.

2. Add the oil, onion, garlic and leek to a shallow casserole dish and bake for 5 minutes.

3. In the meantime, prep the salmon. Create a large foil parcel in a baking dish. Add the frozen salmon fillets and top with the butter, garlic and a little salt and pepper. Fold the foil loosely over the top of the salmon fillets.

4. Remove the casserole dish from the oven and add the risotto rice and hot vegetable stock.

5. Put both dishes, (the risotto and the salmon), into the oven for 25 minutes.

6. After 25 minutes, remove both dishes. Add the frozen peas and grated Parmesan to the risotto and return to the oven for 5 minutes

7. Use a fork to flake the salmon. When the risotto is ready, remove from the oven and mix in the flaked salmon along with any juices.

8. Serve immediately with a side salad or cooked green vegetables.

CREAMY GARLIC & HERB CHICKEN WITH PARMESAN POTATOES

| Serves: 4 | Prep time: 15 minutes | Cook time: 27 minutes | Calories: 400 per portion |

With just a couple of simple ingredients you can create a delicious creamy sauce for chicken. Accompanied by roasted Parmesan cubed potatoes, this dish is packed with flavour but still really healthy.

INGREDIENTS

For the potatoes:
700g baby potatoes

1 tbsp oil

30g grated Parmesan cheese

For the chicken:
2 large (400g) chicken breasts

salt and pepper

½ tbsp oil

165g garlic and herb cream cheese

75ml semi-skimmed milk

To serve:
330g Tenderstem broccoli (or another green vegetable)

STORING:
Leftover chicken and potatoes can be kept in an airtight container in the fridge for up to 2 days.

METHOD

1. Wash the potatoes and, leaving the skins on, cut them into approximately 3cm chunks.

2. Add to a saucepan of boiling water and simmer on high for 5-7 minutes until you can get a knife through them. Be careful not to overcook.

3. In the meantime, preheat the oven to 180°C Fan/200°C/Gas Mark 6.

4. When the potatoes are cooked, drain and add to a large baking tray with the oil and sprinkle the grated Parmesan on top.

5. Bake for 15-20 minutes until crispy.

6. Lay the chicken breasts on a chopping board. You want to slice the chicken breasts through the middle widthways, to make two thinner pieces from each breast, four in total.

7. Season each side of the chicken with a little salt and pepper.

8. Heat the oil in a frying pan and add the chicken.

9. Cook for 4-5 minutes on each side, checking that they are fully cooked in the middle.

10. In the meantime, boil or steam the tenderstem broccoli for 3-4 minutes in a separate saucepan.

11. Add the cream cheese and milk to the chicken and cook for another minute until the cream cheese has melted and created a thick sauce.

12. Divide the chicken and sauce between four plates. Add the roasted potatoes and Tenderstem broccoli and serve immediately.

SESAME-CRUSTED COD TACOS

| Makes: 4 | Prep time: 10 minutes | Cook time: 20 minutes | Calories per portion: 490 |

White fish can often be a little bland and tasteless, but this sesame coating adds bags of flavour. A brilliant meal to serve up family style and let everyone build their own tacos.

INGREDIENTS

For the sesame-crusted cod:

3 skinless cod fillets (approx. 360g)

2 medium eggs

50g panko breadcrumbs

3 tbsp sesame seeds

½ tsp lemon pepper (or ¼ tsp black pepper)

¼ tsp salt

spray oil

For the tacos and salad:

8 mini tortilla wraps

2 little gem lettuce

1 medium carrot

300g cucumber

50g red cabbage

50g tinned sweetcorn

handful fresh coriander

For the sauce:

100g fat-free Greek yogurt

3 tbsp Lighter than Light mayonnaise

2 tbsp tartar sauce

½ tsp garlic powder

METHOD

1. Preheat the oven to 200°C Fan/220°C/Gas Mark 7 and line a baking tray with parchment paper.

2. Crack the eggs into a bowl and whisk with a fork.

3. Add the panko breadcrumbs, sesame seeds, lemon pepper and salt to a large plate and mix well.

4. Take one whole cod fillet, dip it in the egg and then roll in the panko breadcrumb mixture until it is fully coated. Repeat with the remaining two cod fillets.

5. Place the cod fillets on the lined baking tray and spray the top and sides of the fish with spray oil. Bake for 18–20 minutes, ensuring the fish is fully cooked in the middle.

6. In the meantime, prep the tacos and salad. Toast the tortilla wraps in a dry frying pan for 1 minute on either side. Cut the lettuce, red cabbage, carrot and cucumber into thin strips. Place these vegetables, the sweetcorn and the coriander in individual bowls or on one large chopping board.

7. Make the sauce by mixing the yogurt, mayonnaise, tartare sauce and garlic powder together in a bowl.

8. When the fish is cooked, cut the fillets into bite-sized pieces.

SERVING SUGGESTIONS:

Younger children may find this easier if you separate the items out on their plate and cut the tortillas into triangles.

STORING:

This recipe is best eaten immediately after cooking. Leftover fish can be kept in the fridge for up to 2 days, but will lose its crunch.

CAULIFLOWER BOLOGNESE

| Serves: 4 | Prep time: 7 minutes | Cook time: 30 minutes | Calories: 470 (served with pasta and Parmesan) |

This cauliflower Bolognese is a great way to pack lots of veggies into your family's diet. The cauliflower and mushrooms are blitzed into really small pieces, so they aren't noticeable to fussy eaters. It's all super filling too.

INGREDIENTS

1 small cauliflower (approx. 400g)

300g mushrooms

½ tbsp oil

1 onion, diced

2 garlic cloves, crushed

2 carrots, diced

1 celery stick, diced

2 x 400g tins chopped tomatoes

2 tbsp tomato purée

1 tbsp balsamic vinegar

1 tsp dried rosemary

1 tsp dried thyme

salt and pepper

To serve:

350g pasta

50g grated Parmesan cheese

fresh basil leaves

METHOD

1. Chop the cauliflower into small florets and transfer to a food processor. Blitz until the cauliflower reaches rice consistency.

2. Remove the cauliflower from the food processor and add the mushrooms. Blitz until finely chopped.

3. Add the oil and onion to a large frying pan or shallow casserole dish on the hob and cook for 4 minutes.

4. Add the garlic, carrots and celery, along with the blitzed cauliflower and mushrooms and cook for 5 minutes.

5. Add the chopped tomatoes, tomato purée, balsamic vinegar, rosemary and thyme. Season with a little salt and pepper and mix well.

6. Bring to the boil, reduce to a simmer and cook for 20 minutes.

7. In the meantime, cook the pasta according to the package instructions.

8. Serve the Bolognese on top of the cooked pasta and garnish with grated Parmesan and fresh basil.

SERVING SUGGESTIONS:

For children who prefer their food separate, serve the Bolognese and pasta separated on a plate and topped with grated Parmesan.

STORING:

Leftover Bolognese can be kept in an airtight container in the fridge for up to 2 days. It can be frozen for up to 2 months and defrosted in the fridge overnight.

CHICKEN & SPINACH LASAGNE

| Serves: 4 | Prep time: 7 minutes | Cook time: 45 minutes | Calories: 525 (not incl. side salad) |

An alternative to traditional beef lasagne, this recipe is creamy but still light and packed with healthy spinach and courgettes.

INGREDIENTS

2 medium chicken breasts (400g)

½ tbsp oil

1 onion, diced

2 garlic cloves, crushed

1 medium courgette, diced

3 tbsp plain flour

½ tsp dried oregano

500ml semi-skimmed milk

300g frozen chopped spinach

salt and pepper

80g grated Cheddar cheese

30g grated Parmesan cheese

8 lasagne sheets (155g)

100g half-fat crème fraîche

STORING:

Leftover lasagne can be kept in an airtight container in the fridge for up to 2 days. It can also be frozen for up to 2 months and defrosted in the fridge overnight.

METHOD

1. Cut the chicken breasts into thin strips.

2. Add the oil and onion to a large shallow saucepan or casserole dish on the hob and cook on a medium heat for 2 minutes.

3. Add the garlic, courgette and sliced chicken and cook for 5 minutes until the chicken is starting to brown and any juices from the courgette have been cooked off.

4. Add the flour and oregano, stir well and cook for 30 seconds. Next, add the milk and bring to the boil whilst stirring.

5. When the milk starts to thicken, reduce to a low simmer, add the spinach and cook for another 5 minutes. Season with a little salt and pepper.

6. Turn off the heat. Add half of the grated Cheddar and all of the grated Parmesan and mix well.

7. Preheat the oven to 180°C Fan/200°C/Gas Mark 6.

8. Layer the chicken and spinach mixture in an oven dish with the lasagne sheets. I use a 23cm-square dish, starting with a layer of the filling mixture and finishing with a layer of lasagne sheets.

9. Add the crème fraîche on top of the final layer of lasagne sheets and sprinkle on the rest of the Cheddar cheese.

10. Bake for 25 minutes until the lasagne sheets are fully cooked and the cheese has browned.

11. Cut the lasagne into four portions and serve with a side salad.

CRISPY KOREAN BEEF

| Serves: 4 | Prep time: 15 minutes | Cook time: 15 minutes | Calories: 525 per portion |

If you want to try out some new bold flavours with your family, then my crispy beef is perfect. It uses a Korean paste to create a mildly spicy but sweet sauce. Delicious served in crispy lettuce wraps with rice on the side.

INGREDIENTS

For the beef:

400g thin-cut beef steaks

1 medium egg

70g cornflour

1 tsp garlic powder

1 tsp onion powder

salt and pepper

2 tbsp oil

For the veggies:

1 red pepper, sliced

1 yellow pepper, sliced

2 spring onions, chopped

1 cm piece of ginger, peeled and chopped

2 garlic cloves, crushed

For the sauce:

100ml water

2 tbsp soy sauce

2 tbsp ketchup

1 tbsp rice wine vinegar

1 tbsp honey

2 tsp gochujang paste

To serve:

2 packets of microwave rice or 500g cooked rice (165g uncooked rice)

2 little gem lettuce

METHOD

1. Cut the beef into thin strips.

2. Crack the egg into a bowl and whisk with a fork.

3. Add the cornflour, garlic powder, onion powder and salt and pepper to another bowl, and mix well.

4. Take half of the beef strips and add them to the egg. Mix well so that they are completely coated and then transfer to the bowl with the cornflour. Again, mix well so that all the beef strips are fully coated in the cornflour mixture. Repeat with the rest of the beef strips.

5. Heat the oil in a large frying pan on the hob on a medium-high heat. Add half the beef strips and fry for 4-5 minutes until they are cooked through and crispy on the outside.

6. Transfer the cooked beef to a plate and repeat with the remaining strips. Once all the beef is cooked, cover the plate with foil to keep warm.

7. In the same pan, add the peppers, spring onion whites, ginger and garlic and cook for 3 minutes.

8. Add all of the sauce ingredients to a small jug or mug and mix well. Pour the sauce into the pan with the veggies and cook for 1 minute until the sauce starts to thicken.

9. Turn off the heat, add the beef back in and mix well. Prepare the rice.

10. Serve the Korean beef in lettuce leaves along with the rice, garnished with the green of the spring onions.

SERVING SUGGESTIONS:

This recipe is quite mild, so if your children enjoy spicier flavours then, feel free to add more gochujang paste to the sauce. You can also swap this for 1 tbsp sweet chilli sauce if you prefer. For children, you may want to cut the lettuce into small pieces and serve on their plate alongside the rice and beef.

STORING:

This recipe is best eaten immediately after cooking. Leftovers can be kept in the fridge for up to 2 days, but the beef will lose its crispiness.

MEDITERRANEAN SAUSAGE TRAYBAKE

| Serves: 4 | Prep time: 10 minutes | Cook time:35 minutes | Calories: 515 (incl. pitta bread) |

Sausages, vegetables and beans all cooked together in the oven with a tangy Mediterranean sauce. Served with pitta breads which are perfect for dipping!

INGREDIENTS

For the traybake:
spray oil
8 chicken sausages
1 red onion
1 yellow pepper
1 orange pepper
1 medium courgette
150g cherry tomatoes
400g can butter beans, drained
50g pitted black olives

For the sauce:
1 tbsp honey
½ tbsp oil
juice of 1 lemon
½ tsp dried oregano
½ tsp smoked paprika
½ tsp garlic powder
salt and pepper

To serve:
4 pitta breads
handful of fresh basil leaves

METHOD

1. Preheat the oven to 180°C Fan/200°C/Gas Mark 6.

2. Spray a large baking dish with some spray oil and add the chicken sausages. Bake for 10 minutes.

3. In the meantime, prep the veggies. Cut the onion into large chunks. Chop the peppers into large pieces and cut the courgette into rounds. You can leave the cherry tomatoes whole.

4. Add the veggies to the baking dish and mix well.

5. Make the sauce by mixing the honey, oil, lemon juice, oregano, smoked paprika and garlic powder, along with a little salt and pepper, in a small jug or cup. Pour this over the sausages and veggies and mix well.

6. Return to the oven for another 15 minutes.

7. Add the drained butter beans and black olives, mix and cook for a final 10 minutes.

8. Toast the pitta breads and divide the traybake between four bowls, garnished with fresh basil on top.

SERVING SUGGESTIONS:
Sausages can be a choking hazard for young children, so ensure you cut them into four spears before serving.

STORING:
Leftovers can be kept in an airtight container in the fridge for up to 2 days. It can be frozen for up to 2 months and defrosted in the fridge overnight.

BUFFALO & BBQ CHICKEN WINGS WITH BLUE CHEESE DIP

| Serves: 4 | Prep time: 10 minutes | Cook time: 45 minutes | Calories: 610 for Buffalo wings, 635 for BBQ wings incl. dip |

Chicken wings are my ultimate weekend comfort food. My recipe has two versions of a sauce to suit adults and children and uses my secret ingredient, baking powder, for crispy wings that are baked and not fried.

INGREDIENTS

For the chicken wings:

1kg chicken wings

2 tsp baking powder

2 tsp garlic powder

2 tsp onion powder

2 tsp smoked paprika

2 tsp dried oregano

salt and pepper

3 tbsp Frank's Red Hot Buffalo Wings Sauce

3 tbsp BBQ Sauce

For the blue cheese dip:

100g fat-free yogurt

50g Danish blue cheese

1 tbsp semi-skimmed milk

salt and pepper

To serve:

8 celery sticks

> ### STORING:
> These chicken wings are best eaten immediately after cooking. They will, however, keep in the fridge for up to 2 days and can be reheated in the microwave or oven.

METHOD

1. Preheat the oven to 200°C Fan/220°C/ Gas Mark 7.

2. Your wings may already be separated into drummettes and wingettes. If not, cut through the middle of the wing on the bone with a sharp knife to separate.

3. Add the chicken wings to a large bowl with the baking powder and mix well.

4. Add the garlic powder, onion powder, smoked paprika and oregano along with a little salt and pepper and mix again.

5. Transfer the wings to one large or two smaller baking trays and cook for 45 minutes.

6. You can also cook these chicken wings in the air fryer at 200°C for 35 minutes.

7. Once cooked, transfer the wings onto a large plate lined with kitchen roll and pat to remove any excess oil.

8. Divide the wings between two bowls. In one bowl mix in the Buffalo sauce (for the adults). In the other bowl, mix the BBQ sauce (for the kids).

9. Make the blue cheese dip by adding all the ingredients to a small bowl. Mash the blue cheese with a fork to mix it through.

10. Serve the chicken wings with the blue cheese sauce and chopped celery sticks on the side.

VEGGIE ENCHILADA LASAGNE

| Serves: 4 | Prep time: 10 minutes | Cook time: 45 minutes | Calories: 420 (not incl. side salad) |

If you love enchiladas but find rolling them up a faff, or the kids struggle with them, try my enchilada lasagne instead – same great flavour and ingredients, but easier to assemble and eat.

INGREDIENTS

For the lasagne:

½ tbsp oil

1 onion, diced

2 garlic cloves, crushed

2 carrots, diced

1 small courgette, diced

1 red pepper, diced

100g sweetcorn (tinned or frozen)

1 tsp ground cumin

1 tsp smoked paprika

1 tsp dried oregano

½ tsp mild chilli powder

400g tin black beans, drained

400g tin chopped tomatoes

200ml vegetable stock

juice of 1 lime

salt and pepper

3 large tortilla wraps

80g half-fat crème fraîche

1 tbsp milk

75g grated Cheddar cheese

To serve:

handful of fresh coriander

> **STORING:**
> Store leftovers in an airtight container in the fridge for up to 2 days. It can be frozen for up to 2 months and defrosted in the fridge overnight.

METHOD

1. Add the oil and onion to a large saucepan or shallow casserole dish on the hob and cook for 3 minutes. Add the garlic, carrots, courgette, pepper and sweetcorn and cook for another 4 minutes. Then add the cumin, smoked paprika, oregano and mild chilli powder and cook for a further 1 minute.

2. Add the black beans, chopped tomatoes and vegetable stock. Bring to the boil and then simmer on a medium-high heat for 20 minutes.

3. Turn off the heat and add the lime juice, along with a little salt and pepper.

4. Preheat the oven to 200°C Fan/220°C/ Gas Mark 7. You will need a square baking dish approximately 23cm for the lasagne.

5. Add a third of the enchilada mixture to the bottom of the tin, followed by one of the tortilla wraps. Add a second layer of the mixture, another wrap and then finally the remaining enchilada mixture. On top add the last tortilla wrap. When layering the tortilla wraps, tuck them up the sides of the dish, rather than trim them.

6. In a bowl or jug, mix together the crème fraîche and milk. Pour this over the top of the lasagne and then add the grated cheese. Bake for 15–18 minutes until the cheese has browned.

7. Cut the lasagne into four portions and serve on a plate garnished with a little chopped coriander. Add a side salad or crudités.

TANDOORI CHICKEN DRUMSTICKS

| Serves: 4 | Prep time: 10 minutes, plus 1 hour to marinate | Cook time: 45 minutes | Calories: 620 (not incl. side salad) |

Chicken drumsticks are great for kids who prefer finger food. My recipe uses a tandoori marinade to add lots of flavour, with just a hint of mild spice. Serve it up with a cooling raita dip.

INGREDIENTS

For the drumsticks:

12 chicken drumsticks (1.4kg)

300g fat-free Greek yogurt

3 tbsp tandoori powder

1 tbsp mango chutney

1 garlic clove, crushed

1cm piece of ginger, peeled and chopped

juice of 1 lemon

salt and pepper

For the raita:

150g fat-free Greek yogurt

50g cucumber, finely chopped

1 tsp mint sauce

½ tsp garlic powder

¼ tsp garam masala

salt and pepper

To serve:

chopped fresh coriander

2 packets microwave pilau rice
or 500g cooked rice (165g uncooked rice)

METHOD

1. Remove the skin from the chicken drumsticks and, using a sharp knife, make four or five slits in the meat of each one.

2. In a large bowl, add the yogurt, tandoori powder, mango chutney, garlic, ginger and lemon juice. Mix well and season with a little salt and pepper. Add the chicken drumsticks to the bowl and mix so that they are all coated in the marinade.

3. Cover and leave in the fridge for at least an hour. I usually do this in the morning or the night before.

4. Preheat the oven to 200°C Fan/220°C/Gas Mark 7. Transfer the chicken drumsticks into a large baking dish and bake in the oven for 45 minutes.

5. Make the raita by mixing together the yogurt, cucumber, mint sauce, garlic powder and garam masala. Season with a little salt and pepper.

6. Cook the rice in the microwave according to the package instructions.

7. Remove the drumsticks from the oven and check that they are fully cooked in the middle. Serve the drumsticks garnished with a little chopped coriander and with the microwave pilau rice, raita and a side salad.

SERVING SUGGESTIONS:

Younger children may find this easier to eat if you remove the chicken meat from the drumsticks for them.

STORING:

Leftover drumsticks can be kept in the fridge for up to 2 days and reheated in the microwave or oven.

BAKED CHORIZO RICE

 NF

| Serves: 4 | Prep time: 7 minutes | Cook time: 35 minutes | Calories: 465 per portion (not incl. side salad or vegetables) |

A simple but flavourful Spanish rice dish, all cooked in the oven.

INGREDIENTS

½ tbsp oil

1 onion, diced

2 garlic cloves, crushed

100g chorizo, chopped

300g easy-cook long-grain white rice

1 litre vegetable stock

1 yellow pepper, chopped

¼ tsp smoked paprika

¼ tsp ground turmeric

100g frozen peas

50g pitted black olives

To serve:

juice of ½ lemon

fresh parsley

> **STORING:**
> Leftovers can be kept in an airtight container in the fridge for up to 2 days. It can be frozen for up to 2 months and defrosted in the fridge overnight.

METHOD

1. Preheat the oven to 180°C Fan/200°C/Gas Mark 6.

2. Add the oil, onion, garlic and chorizo to a large shallow casserole dish and mix well.

3. Bake for 10 minutes.

4. Add the rice, vegetable stock, yellow pepper, smoked paprika and turmeric and return to the oven for a further 20 minutes, stirring twice.

5. Add the frozen peas and olives and cook for a final 5 minutes.

6. Remove from the oven and squeeze on the lemon juice.

7. Divide between four plates or bowls, garnished with chopped fresh parsley.

8. Serve with a side salad or cooked green vegetables.

SOUPS, STEWS & CASSEROLES

Creamy Chicken Casserole
Spanish Cod Stew
Cajun Beef & Vegetable Casserole
Louisiana Gumbo
Gyoza Noodle Soup
Roasted Vegetable Soup
Cauliflower Cheese Soup
Mexican Tomato Soup
Tortellini Minestrone
Miso Soup

CREAMY CHICKEN CASSEROLE

| Serves: 4 | Prep time: 5 minutes | Cook time: 35 minutes | Calories: 335 per portion (not incl. potato or rice) |

This chicken casserole is the ultimate bowl of comfort on a cold evening. Serve just as it is for a light meal and add a baked potato or rice to make it more substantial.

INGREDIENTS

1 tbsp oil

600g (3 medium) chicken breasts, diced

1 onion, diced

2 garlic cloves, crushed

2 carrots, finely diced

1 leek, sliced into rounds

1 celery stick, diced

3 tbsp plain flour

800ml chicken stock

2 tsp Dijon mustard

½ tsp dried thyme

½ tsp dried rosemary

100g frozen peas

75g light cream cheese

STORING:

This casserole can be kept in an airtight container in the fridge for up to 2 days and reheated on the hob or in the microwave. It can be frozen for up to 2 months and defrosted in the fridge overnight.

METHOD

1. Add half the oil (½ tablespoon) to a large casserole dish along with the diced chicken breast and cook on the hob for 4-5 minutes until the chicken is starting to brown.

2. Remove the chicken from the pan and set aside in a bowl.

3. Add the remaining oil to the pan along with the onion, garlic, carrots, leek and celery.

4. Cook for 4 minutes until the vegetables are starting to soften.

5. Add the flour, mix well and cook for 30 seconds.

6. Add the chicken stock, Dijon mustard, thyme and rosemary. Mix well and add back in the partly cooked chicken.

7. Bring to the boil, reduce to a simmer and cook for 20 minutes until the chicken and vegetables are fully cooked.

8. Add the frozen peas and cream cheese, mix well and cook for a further 4 minutes.

9. Serve immediately on its own or with baked potato or rice.

SPANISH COD STEW

| Serves: 4 | Prep time: 6 minutes | Cook time: 18 minutes | Calories: 200 (without pitta bread) |

Although this recipe is called a stew, the ingredients make it really light and summery.
Perfect for a lighter meal on warmer days.

INGREDIENTS

½ tbsp oil

1 onion, diced

2 garlic cloves, crushed

1 yellow pepper, sliced

100g cherry tomatoes

70g pitted black olives

30g capers

2 x 400g tins chopped tomatoes

½ tsp dried oregano

½ tsp smoked paprika

salt and pepper

3 fillets (300g) frozen white fish
(cod, haddock, pollock, hake etc.)

100g large frozen prawns

juice of ½ lemon

To serve:

chopped fresh parsley

toasted pitta breads

METHOD

1. Add the oil and onion to a large, shallow casserole dish on the hob and cook for 3 minutes.

2. Add the garlic and cook for another 1 minute.

3. Add the yellow pepper, cherry tomatoes, olives, capers, tinned tomatoes, oregano and smoked paprika. Season with a little salt and pepper and mix well.

4. Add the frozen fish fillets and cook on a medium simmer for 5 minutes.

5. Turn the fish over and add the frozen prawns.

6. Cook for a further 5-7 minutes, checking to ensure that the fish and prawns are fully cooked through.

7. Stir in the lemon juice and sprinkle some chopped fresh parsley on top.

8. Serve immediately on its own or with some toasted pitta breads (use gluten-free bread if needed).

> ## STORING:
> This stew can be kept in an airtight container in the fridge for up to 2 days and reheated on the hob or in the microwave.

CAJUN BEEF & VEGETABLE CASSEROLE

| Serves: 4 | Prep time: 10 minutes | Cook time: 1 hour 10 mins | Calories: 400 per portion (not incl. bread roll) |

Upgrade a classic beef casserole with some simple Cajun seasoning. It adds lots of new flavour and lightens up the dish to make it less heavy, ideal for a warming meal all year round.

INGREDIENTS

400g lean diced beef

3 tbsp plain flour

1 tbsp oil

1 onion, diced

600g Maris Piper potatoes

2 carrots

1 leek

250g frozen butternut squash chunks

200g button mushrooms

2 garlic cloves, crushed

800ml beef stock

2 tbsp tomato purée

2 tsp Cajun seasoning

1 tsp smoked paprika

salt and pepper

To serve:
chopped fresh parsley

STORING:

This casserole can be kept in an airtight container in the fridge for up to 2 days and reheated on the hob or in the microwave. It can be frozen for up to 2 months and defrosted in the fridge overnight.

METHOD

1. Preheat the oven to 180°C Fan/200°C/Gas Mark 6. For this recipe you will need a large casserole dish with a lid.

2. Add the diced beef and flour to a bowl and mix.

3. Heat the oil on a medium heat on the hob in the casserole dish and add the beef.

4. Cook for 4 minutes until the beef has browned.

5. Add the onion and cook for another 2 minutes. Whilst the beef and onions are cooking, prep the veggies. Peel the potatoes and chop them into three or four medium-sized chunks each. Peel the carrots and chop them into thin rounds. Cut the leek into thick rounds.

6. When the beef and onions have finished cooking, turn off the heat and add the potatoes, carrots and leek along with the frozen butternut squash, mushrooms and garlic. Stir well.

7. Add the stock, tomato purée, Cajun seasoning and smoked paprika to a large jug. Season with a little salt and pepper and mix well. Pour this over the beef and vegetables and mix.

8. Put the lid on the casserole dish and cook in the oven for 1 hour, stirring a couple of times.

9. Check the potatoes and carrots are cooked. You should be able to get a knife through them easily. If not, return to the oven for another 10 minutes.

10. Garnish with parsley and serve immediately, either on its own or with a small bread roll.

LOUISIANA GUMBO

| Serves: 4 | Prep time: 6 minutes | Cook time: 21 minutes | Calories: 195 (without bread rolls) |

This gumbo is hearty and filling without being heavy and stodgy. Traditional gumbo uses okra but it's not always easy to find, so I have used green beans instead. Feel free to substitute for okra if you prefer!

INGREDIENTS

½ tbsp oil

1 onion, diced

4 (approx. 130g) lean smoked bacon medallions, chopped

2 garlic cloves, crushed

½ tsp dried thyme

½ tsp dried oregano

¼ tsp cayenne pepper or smoked paprika

¼ tsp ground turmeric

2 tbsp tomato purée

1 red pepper, chopped

1 celery stick, chopped

1 litre chicken stock (use gluten-free)

100g basmati rice

150g frozen large prawns

100g green beans, halved

METHOD

1. Add the oil and onion to a large saucepan and cook for 3 minutes.

2. Add the bacon and garlic and cook for another 2 minutes.

3. Add the thyme, oregano, cayenne pepper, turmeric and tomato purée. Stir well and cook for a further 1 minute.

4. Add the red pepper, celery and chicken stock and bring to the boil.

5. Add the rice and cook on a high simmer for 7 minutes.

6. Add the frozen prawns and green beans and cook for another 5 minutes.

7. Serve immediately on its own or with crusty bread rolls.

> ### STORING:
> This gumbo can be kept in an airtight container in the fridge for up to 2 days and reheated on the hob or in the microwave.

GYOZA NOODLE SOUP

| Serves: 4 | Prep time: 2 minutes | Cook time: 10 minutes | Calories: 335 per portion |

I always have a packet of pre-made gyoza in the freezer, ready to whip up this simple noodle soup on busy days. It's quick and easy to make and packed with delicious Japanese flavours.

INGREDIENTS

2 garlic cloves, crushed

1 cm piece of ginger, peeled and chopped

2 litres hot vegetable stock

2 tbsp soy sauce

200g dried rice noodles

16 frozen vegetable gyoza

200g Tenderstem broccoli

200g pak choi

To serve:

2 spring onions, chopped

1 red chilli, sliced and deseeded

METHOD

1. Add the garlic, ginger, vegetable stock, soy sauce and rice noodles to a large saucepan on the hob.

2. Simmer on high for 5 minutes.

3. Add the gyoza, broccoli and pak choi and continue to cook for another 5 minutes.

4. Divide between four bowls and garnish with spring onions and sliced chilli for adults.

SERVING SUGGESTIONS:

For children who are not big fans of soup, you can remove the noodles, gyoza and vegetables and serve just a small portion of them both on the side.

STORING:

This soup can be kept in an airtight container in the fridge for up to 2 days and reheated on the hob or in the microwave.

ROASTED VEGETABLE SOUP

| Serves: 4 | Prep time: 10 minutes | Cook time: 45 minutes | Calories: 220 per portion, served as a soup |

This soup is a brilliant way to use up vegetables that may be a little past their best and not great to eat fresh. It's super filling but can also be used as a pasta sauce for fussy eaters.

INGREDIENTS

1 red onion

2 garlic cloves

1 red pepper

1 yellow pepper

2 carrots

1 medium courgette

1 aubergine

300g tomatoes

2 tbsp olive oil

1 tsp smoked paprika

1 tsp dried oregano

700ml vegetable stock

400g tin chopped tomatoes

salt and pepper

To serve:

40g grated Parmesan

fresh basil leaves

METHOD

1. Preheat the oven to 200°C Fan/220°C/Gas Mark 7.

2. Chop the onion into chunks and crush the garlic. Cut the carrots, courgette and aubergine into thin rounds. Roughly chop the peppers into chunks. Chop the tomatoes into quarters.

3. Add the vegetables to a large roasting tray along with the oil, paprika and oregano and mix well.

4. Cook in the oven for 30 minutes.

5. When the vegetables are cooked, transfer them to a large saucepan on the hob.

6. Add the vegetable stock and tinned tomatoes. Season with a little salt and pepper.

7. Bring to the boil, reduce to a simmer and cook for a further 10 minutes.

8. Blitz with a hand blender until smooth. If the soup is a little too thick for your liking, add a splash of water to thin it out.

SERVING SUGGESTIONS:

Serve to adults as a soup topped with a little grated Parmesan and fresh basil leaves. For kids, serve as a pasta sauce. Simply mix with cooked pasta and top with grated Parmesan.

STORING:

This soup can be kept in an airtight container in the fridge for up to 2 days and reheated on the hob or in the microwave. It can be frozen for up to 2 months and defrosted in the fridge overnight.

CAULIFLOWER CHEESE SOUP

| Serves: 4 | Prep time: 5 minutes | Cook time:20 minutes | Calories: 285 per portion, served as a soup |

All the great flavours of a classic cauliflower cheese, but served up as a warming soup. This is another recipe that works really well as a pasta sauce too.

INGREDIENTS

1 tbsp butter

1 onion, diced

2 garlic cloves, crushed

1 medium cauliflower (450g)

250g potatoes

500ml vegetable stock

500ml semi-skimmed milk

½ tsp dried oregano

70g grated Cheddar cheese

30g grated Parmesan

1 tsp Dijon mustard

salt and pepper

To serve:

chopped fresh chives

SERVING SUGGESTIONS:

Serve as a soup to adults, garnished with some chopped chives. For kids, serve as a pasta sauce. Simply mix with cooked pasta and top with a little grated cheese.

STORING:

This soup can be kept in an airtight container in the fridge for up to 2 days and reheated on the hob or in the microwave. It can be frozen for up to 2 months and defrosted in the fridge overnight.

METHOD

1. Add the butter and onion to a large saucepan on the hob and cook for 3 minutes.

2. Add the garlic and cook for 1 minute.

3. Remove the leaves and stalk from the cauliflower and cut into large chunks.

4. Leaving the skins on the potatoes, cut them into smaller chunks.

5. Add the cauliflower and potatoes to the saucepan along with the vegetable stock, milk and oregano.

6. Bring to the boil and simmer for 12–15 minutes until the vegetables are soft.

7. Remove the saucepan from the heat and blitz with a hand blender until the soup is smooth.

8. Stir in the Cheddar cheese, Parmesan and Dijon mustard until completely melted.

9. Season to taste with a little salt and pepper. If the soup is a little too thick for your liking, add a splash of water to thin it out.

MEXICAN TOMATO SOUP

| Serves: 4 | Prep time: 3 minutes | Cook time: 20 minutes | Calories: 230 per portion |

My kids love a simple tomato soup, but this Mexican version upgrades it to make it a bit more exciting. It's also really fun to serve up with all the toppings.

INGREDIENTS

½ tbsp oil

1 onion, diced

2 garlic cloves, crushed

½ tsp ground cumin

½ tsp ground coriander

½ tsp smoked paprika

¼ tsp mild chilli powder

150g potatoes

400g tin chopped tomatoes

1 litre vegetable stock

salt and pepper

To serve:

80g grated cheddar cheese

50g tortilla chips

1 lime, cut into quarters

handful of fresh coriander

METHOD

1. Add the oil and onion to a large saucepan on the hob and cook on a medium heat for 2 minutes.

2. Add the garlic, cumin, ground coriander, smoked paprika and chilli powder. Mix well and cook for another 1 minute.

3. Leaving the skins on, chop the potatoes into small bite-sized pieces and add these to the saucepan along with the chopped tomatoes and vegetable stock. Season with a little salt and pepper.

4. Bring to the boil, reduce to a simmer and cook for another 12 minutes.

5. Blitz the soup with a hand blender until completely smooth.

6. Divide between four bowls and top with grated cheddar, tortilla chips, a lime quarter and some fresh coriander.

SERVING SUGGESTIONS:

For children, you may want to serve the toppings on the side and let them add them themselves.

STORING:

This soup can be kept in an airtight container in the fridge for up to 2 days without the toppings and reheated on the hob or in the microwave. It can be frozen for up to 2 months and defrosted in the fridge overnight.

TORTELLINI MINESTRONE

| Serves: 4 | Prep time: 5 minutes | Cook time: 25 minutes | Calories: 260 per portion (not incl. bread roll) |

Turn a packet of supermarket tortellini into a hearty minestrone soup. Serve on its own or add a bread roll for a more substantial meal.

INGREDIENTS

½ tbsp oil

1 onion, diced

2 garlic cloves, crushed

1 medium carrot, finely diced

1 celery stick, diced

1 red pepper, diced

2 x 400g tins chopped tomatoes

600ml vegetable stock

salt and pepper

300g spinach and ricotta tortellini

To serve:

fresh basil leaves

crusty bread rolls

METHOD

1. Add the oil and onion to a large saucepan on the hob and cook for 2 minutes.

2. Add the garlic, carrot, celery and red pepper and cook for another 2 minutes.

3. Add the chopped tomatoes and vegetable stock and season with a little salt and pepper.

4. Bring to the boil and simmer on a medium heat for 12 minutes or until the carrot is soft.

5. Add the tortellini and cook for a final 3-4 minutes.

6. Divide between four bowls and garnish with fresh basil leaves.

7. Serve on its own or with crusty bread rolls.

> ### STORING:
> This soup can be kept in an airtight container in the fridge for up to 2 days and reheated on the hob or in the microwave. It can be frozen (with the tortellini in it) for up to 2 months and defrosted in the fridge overnight.

MISO SOUP

| Serves: 4 | Prep time: 1 minutes | Cook time: 7 minutes | Calories: 25 per portion |

During the winter, I regularly drink this miso soup during the day instead of another cup of tea or coffee. It also works brilliantly as a base for any Japanese-style soups.

INGREDIENTS

2 garlic cloves, crushed

1 cm piece of ginger, peeled and chopped

2 tsp miso paste

1 litre vegetable stock

METHOD

1. Put all the ingredients in a saucepan on the hob.

2. Bring to the boil and then simmer for 5 minutes.

3. Serve immediately in mugs.

SERVING SUGGESTIONS:

This may not be to most children's tastes, and that's OK. My children don't enjoy it, but it's worth serving them up a very small cup every now and then to help develop their tastes a little further.

STORING:

This soup can be kept in an airtight container in the fridge for up to 3 days and reheated on the hob or in the microwave. It can be frozen for up to 2 months and defrosted in the fridge overnight.

SALADS & SIDES

Chargrilled Courgettes with Lemon, Mint & Feta
Spring Roll Salad
Rainbow Coleslaw
Cheesy Garlic Bread
Two Ingredient Naan
Greek Salad
Everyday Chopped Salad
Spinach & Strawberry Salad
Patatas Bravas
Chorizo Potato Salad

CHARGRILLED COURGETTES WITH LEMON, MINT & FETA

   GF EF NF V

| Serves: 4 | Prep time: 2 minutes | Cook time: 12 | Calories: 100 per portion |

This courgette side dish is the perfect accompaniment to simple chicken or fish dishes. It's also delicious served up for lunch (have a double portion) with toasted bread.

INGREDIENTS

2 courgettes

1 tbsp oil

½ tsp dried oregano

¼ tsp chilli flakes

salt and pepper

juice of 1 lemon

6 sprigs of fresh mint, chopped

80g feta, chopped into small cubes

STORING:

This salad tastes best eaten immediately after cooking; however, leftovers will keep in the fridge in an airtight container for up to 2 days.

METHOD

1. Remove the top and tail of each courgette.

2. Cut the courgettes into six long slices each, lengthways. I find this easier by cutting them into thirds first and then cut each of those thirds in half. You should have twelve long slices of courgette.

3. Add the courgette slices to a plate along with the oil, oregano, chilli flakes and a little salt and pepper and mix well. You can leave the chilli flakes off any portion for the children.

4. Add the courgette slices to a grill pan and cook for 2-3 minutes on either side. You will probably have to do this in two batches.

5. Add the cooked courgette back to the plate that you used previously. Pour on the lemon juice, add the chopped fresh mint and mix well.

6. Serve with cubes of feta on top.

SPRING ROLL SALAD

All the flavours of spring rolls, but in a healthy bowl of salad. A tasty side dish
to any Southeast-Asian-style meals.

INGREDIENTS

For the salad:

spray oil

1 pack of stir-fry vegetable mix
(approx. 320g)

handful of fresh coriander

For the dressing:

1 tbsp soy sauce

1 tbsp honey

½ tbsp rice wine vinegar

juice of ½ lime

½ tsp garlic powder

> ### STORING:
> This salad tastes best eaten
> immediately after cooking; however,
> leftovers will keep in the fridge in an
> airtight container for up to 2 days.

METHOD

1. Heat some spray oil in a wok and add the stir-fry vegetable mix.

2. Cook for 2 minutes, stirring constantly. You want to cook the vegetables ever so slightly but not as much as you usually would when stir-frying them.

3. Remove the vegetables from the wok and place in a bowl to cool.

4. In the meantime, make the dressing by mixing all the ingredients together in a small bowl.

5. When the vegetables have cooled, add some chopped fresh coriander, pour on the dressing and mix well.

6. Serve immediately.

RAINBOW COLESLAW

| Serves: 4 | Prep time: 5 minutes | Cook time: none | Calories: 50 per portion |

Shop-bought coleslaw can often be very heavy and laden with mayonnaise. This homemade version is light and fresh, using a garlic crème fraîche instead.

INGREDIENTS

100g red cabbage

100g white cabbage

2 spring onions

1 medium carrot

handful of fresh parsley

70g half-fat crème fraîche

juice of ½ lemon

¼ tsp garlic powder

salt and pepper

STORING:

This salad tastes best eaten immediately after preparing; however, leftovers will keep in the fridge in an airtight container for up to 24 hours.

METHOD

1. Chop the red and white cabbage into small, thin strips.

2. Cut the spring onions into rounds and coarsely grate the carrot.

3. Finely chop the fresh parsley and put all the vegetables in a large bowl.

4. In a small bowl, mix together the crème fraîche, lemon juice, garlic powder and season with a little salt and pepper.

5. Pour this over the vegetables and mix again.

6. Serve immediately. If you want to make this coleslaw ahead of time, keep the vegetables and sauce in separate bowls and mix when ready to serve.

CHEESY GARLIC BREAD

| Serves: 4 | Prep time: 1 minute | Cook time: 4 minutes | Calories: 210 per portion |

Cheesy garlic bread is my ultimate comfort food. This homemade version is so easy to make in just five minutes, and healthier than the shop-bought version too.

INGREDIENTS

4 mini tortilla wraps
20g (4 tsp) butter
1 tsp garlic powder
80g grated Cheddar cheese
handful of fresh parsley

STORING:
This garlic bread is best eaten immediately after cooking.

METHOD

1. Place the wrap under the grill for 2 minutes. Don't have it too near the element. Let it get crispy but be careful not to burn it.

2. Mix the butter and garlic powder together in a small bowl.

3. When the wrap is crispy on one side, turn it over and spread on the garlic butter, then add the grated cheese on top.

4. Place it back under the grill for another 2 minutes.

5. Garnish with chopped fresh parsley and serve immediately.

TWO INGREDIENT NAAN

| Makes: 4 | Prep time: 4 minutes | Cook time: 12 minutes | Calories: 155 per portion |

This is a great recipe to get the kids involved in making: homemade naan using just flour and yogurt.

INGREDIENTS

150g self-raising flour
100g fat-free Greek yogurt
pinch of salt
½ tbsp oil

STORING:
These naan are best eaten warm immediately after cooking.

METHOD

1. Add the flour, yogurt and salt to a large bowl and mix well. (These naan are plain but you can also add flavour in the form of garlic, herbs or spices. Just add to the dough when mixing.)

2. Once it has formed a ball of dough, divide into four pieces.

3. Add a little flour to your surface and form each dough piece into a naan shape. Roll out to make it as thin as possible. The dough will rise as it cooks so it's important to get it very thin.

4. Heat the oil in a grill pan or frying pan and add the naan.

5. Cook for 3 minutes on one side, flip and then cook for a further 3 minutes on the other side. You may have to do this in two batches.

6. Serve immediately as a side dish.

GREEK SALAD

| Serves: 4 | Prep time: 5 minutes | Cook time: none | Calories: 150 per portion |

I never used to put capers in a Greek salad until I went on holiday to Crete last year.
They add a tasty salty tang and now are an absolute must for me!

INGREDIENTS

For the salad:

3 vine tomatoes

160g cucumber

½ red onion

70g pitted green olives

1 tbsp capers

100g feta

For the dressing:

1 tbsp olive oil

¼ tsp garlic powder

¼ tsp dried oregano

salt and pepper

METHOD

1. Chop the tomatoes into wedges. Cut the cucumber in half lengthways and then chop into half-moon shapes. Slice the red onion into half rings. Cut the olives in half lengthways.

2. Add all these ingredients to a bowl with the capers and mix well.

3. Cut the feta into small cubes and add on top.

4. Mix the dressing ingredients together and pour over the salad.

5. Serve immediately.

SERVING SUGGESTIONS:

For kids you might want to serve the salad ingredients separated and perhaps without the dressing if they would prefer. Grating the feta is also a really gentle way to introduce this stronger flavour of cheese to younger children.

STORING:

This salad will keep in the fridge in an airtight container for up to 2 days.

EVERYDAY CHOPPED SALAD

| Serves: 4 | Prep time: 5 minutes | Cook time: none | Calories: 100 per portion |

I called this recipe my Everyday Chopped Salad as I could literally eat it every day. All the ingredients are chopped up really small, making it really easy to eat as well. You could also serve it up for lunch by adding a protein source, such as cooked chicken, cheese or chickpeas.

INGREDIENTS

For the salad:

2 sweet gem lettuce

2 spring onions

1 yellow pepper

100g cucumber

100g cherry tomatoes

50g pitted green olives

40g sun-dried tomatoes

For the dressing:

2 tsp olive oil

2 tsp white wine vinegar

2 tsp honey

2 tsp Dijon mustard

salt and pepper

METHOD

1. Chop all the salad ingredients into small, bite-sized pieces. Add to a large bowl.

2. Add the dressing ingredients to a small bowl and mix well.

3. Pour the dressing over the salad, toss and serve.

> ### STORING:
> This salad is best eaten immediately after preparing; however, leftovers will keep in the fridge for up to 2 days.

SPINACH & STRAWBERRY SALAD

| Serves: 4 | Prep time: 4 minutes | Cook time: none | Calories: 65 per portion |

I'm not usually a big fan of fruit in salads, but the balsamic vinegar in this dressing really brings out the sweetness of the strawberries and baby spinach. Light, fresh and super healthy. Give it a try!

INGREDIENTS

100g fresh baby spinach

1 tbsp olive oil

1 tbsp balsamic vinegar

1 tbsp honey

½ tsp Dijon mustard

salt and pepper

200g strawberries

STORING:
This salad will keep in the fridge in an airtight container for up to 2 days.

METHOD

1. Add the baby spinach to a large bowl.

2. Mix the olive oil, balsamic vinegar, honey and Dijon mustard together in a small bowl. Season with salt and pepper.

3. Pour the dressing over the spinach leaves and toss.

4. Slice the strawberries and add these to the top.

5. Serve immediately.

PATATAS BRAVAS

| Serves: 4 | Prep time: 14 minutes | Cook time: 25 minutes | Calories: 250 per portion |

This Spanish dish is perfect for adding a carb-rich side to lots of main meals.
It's also super tasty just as a snack.

INGREDIENTS

For the potatoes:

800g baby potatoes

2 tbsp oil

For the bravas sauce:

400g tin chopped tomatoes

½ tsp garlic powder

½ tsp onion powder

½ tsp smoked paprika

¼ tsp mild chilli powder

salt and pepper

For the garlic sauce:

150g fat-free Greek yogurt

1 tsp garlic powder

juice of ½ lemon

salt and pepper

To garnish:

chopped fresh parsley

METHOD

1. Preheat the oven to 200°C Fan/220°C/Gas Mark 7 and line a large baking tray with parchment paper.

2. Leaving the skins on, cut the potatoes into cubes approximately 2cm in size.

3. Add to a large bowl of cold water and leave to soak for 10 minutes.

4. After 10 minutes, drain the potatoes and add them back into the bowl with the oil and mix well.

5. Add the potatoes to the lined baking tray and bake for 20-25 minutes until they are cooked through and crispy on the outside.

6. In the meantime, make the sauces.

7. Add all the ingredients for the bravas sauce to a blender or food processor and blitz until smooth.

8. For the garlic sauce, add the ingredients to a bowl and mix well.

9. When the potatoes are cooked, remove from the oven and serve either with the sauces drizzled on top (or served separately for children).

10. Garnish with a little chopped fresh parsley.

STORING:

The potatoes are best eaten warm immediately after cooking; however, leftovers will keep in the fridge for up to 2 days. Leftover sauce can be stored in the fridge for up to 3 days. It can be frozen for up to 2 months and defrosted in the fridge overnight.

CHORIZO POTATO SALAD

| Serves: 4 | Prep time: 5 minutes | Cook time: 23 minutes | Calories: 220 per portion |

This potato salad recipe is lighter as it doesn't use mayonnaise, instead using the oils of the chorizo to coat and flavour the salad.

INGREDIENTS

800g baby potatoes

75g chorizo

1 tbsp chopped fresh chives

salt and pepper

> **STORING:**
> This potato salad will keep in the fridge in an airtight container for up to 2 days.

METHOD

1. Wash the baby potatoes and cut them into large chunks, leaving the skins on.

2. Add them to a large saucepan on the hob with cold water and a little salt.

3. Bring to the boil, reduce to a simmer and cook for 10 minutes.

4. You will know the potatoes are cooked when you are able to get a sharp knife through them easily, but don't overcook them so that they are very soft.

5. Drain the potatoes, run them under cold water to cool and set aside.

6. Chop the chorizo into small pieces and add it to the saucepan that you cooked the potatoes in.

7. Fry on low for 6-7 minutes until the oils have been released and the chorizo is crispy.

8. Add the potatoes back in to the saucepan, along with the chives and season to taste with a little salt and pepper. Mix well.

9. Serve immediately as a side dish.

SNACKS & DESSERTS

Blueberry Lemon Cheesecake Bars
Chocolate Fudge Cake Bars
Apple & Blueberry Crumble
Orange & Coconut Cake
Raspberry & White Chocolate Cookies
Lemon Loaf
Chocolate Popcorn
Chocolate Orange Hot Choc
Banoffee Mess
Carrot Cake Muffins
Chocolate Granola Bars
Chocolate Mousse
Mango Sorbet
Affogato & Kiddies' Affogato

BLUEBERRY LEMON CHEESECAKE BARS

| Makes: 12 | Prep time: 12 minutes | Cook time: 25 mins, plus 1 hour freezing time | Calories: 170 per bar |

All the delicious flavour of a cheesecake but made lighter and healthier. A great dessert to get the kids involved with making too.

INGREDIENTS

150g digestive biscuits

50g butter, melted

360g light cream cheese

150g fat-free Greek yogurt

50g white sugar

1 medium egg

2 tsp vanilla extract

juice of ½ lemon

150g fresh blueberries

STORING:

This cheesecake can be kept in an airtight container in the fridge for up to 2 days.

METHOD

1. Preheat the oven to 180°C Fan/200°C/Gas Mark 6 and line a brownie tin (approximately 23cm square) with parchment paper.

2. Put the digestive biscuits in a food processor and blitz. Alternatively, you can crush them in a plastic food bag. Seal tight and bash with a rolling pin.

3. Add the melted butter and blitz again.

4. Press the biscuit mixture into the bottom of the lined tin and bake for 8 minutes.

5. Rinse out the food processor and add the cream cheese, yogurt, sugar, egg, vanilla extract and lemon juice. Blitz until smooth. This can also be done by hand in a bowl.

6. Add half the blueberries and blitz for a final few seconds.

7. Stir in the remaining blueberries by hand to keep them whole.

8. Pour this into the tin on top of the cooked biscuit base. Spread it out evenly, but be careful not to break up the biscuit mixture.

9. Bake for 25 minutes.

10. When cooked, leave in the tin to cool, then transfer to the freezer to set for 1 hour.

11. Cut into twelve bars.

CHOCOLATE FUDGE CAKE BARS

| Makes: 9 cake bars | Prep time: 5 minutes | Cook time: 15 minutes | Calories: 200 per portion |

Soft and fudgy, these bars are a cross between a brownie and chocolate cake. They're super easy to make too, in just one bowl with no other equipment needed.

INGREDIENTS

300g fat-free Greek yogurt

100g white sugar

2 medium eggs

80g butter, melted

2 tsp vanilla extract

100g plain flour

40g cocoa powder

1 tsp bicarbonate of soda

STORING:

These cake bars can be kept in an airtight container in the fridge for up to 2 days, or frozen in freezer bags for up to 3 months and defrosted at room temperature in 2 hours.

METHOD

1. Preheat the oven to 180°C Fan/200°C/Gas Mark 6 and line a brownie tin (approximately 23cm square) with parchment paper.

2. Add the yogurt, sugar, eggs, melted butter and vanilla to a large bowl and mix well.

3. Add the flour, cocoa powder and bicarbonate of soda and mix just enough so that all the ingredients are well combined.

4. Pour the mixture into the lined tin and bake for 15 minutes.

5. Allow the cake to cool a little before cutting into nine pieces.

APPLE & BLUEBERRY CRUMBLE

| Serves: 4 | Prep time: 5 minutes | Cook time: 44 minutes | Calories: 265 per portion |

Crumble is the ultimate comfort food dessert. This version is lighter and healthier than usual, but still just as tasty.

INGREDIENTS

3 medium (400g) red apples

1 tbsp honey

juice of 1 orange or 100ml carton orange juice

50g plain flour

20g porridge oats

20g sugar

30g cold butter

100g fresh blueberries

To serve:

400g fat-free Greek yogurt

1 tsp vanilla extract

STORING:

This crumble can be kept in the fridge for up to 2 days or frozen for up to 3 months and defrosted in the fridge overnight and reheated.

METHOD

1. Preheat the oven to 180°C Fan/200°C/Gas Mark 6.

2. Peel the apples, remove the core and chop them into small, bite-sized pieces.

3. Add the chopped apples to a saucepan with the honey and orange juice.

4. Cook on the hob for 7-9 minutes until you can get a sharp knife through the apples.

5. In the meantime, make the crumble topping by mixing the flour, oats and sugar in a bowl.

6. Add the butter and rub it into the flour mixture with your fingers.

7. When the apples are cooked, transfer them to a small baking dish.

8. Add the blueberries and then top with the crumble mixture. (The blueberries can be substituted for other berries such as blackberries, strawberries or raspberries.)

9. Bake in the oven for 30-35 minutes until the top is golden brown.

10. Divide the crumble between four small bowls.

11. Mix together the yogurt and vanilla and serve on top of the crumble.

ORANGE & COCONUT CAKE

| Serves: 12 | Prep time: 6 minutes | Cook time: 22 minutes | Calories: 185 per slice |

This cake is easy to make with no special equipment or mixers needed. The cake is spongy, and the topping is light and creamy. The perfect Sunday afternoon treat!

INGREDIENTS

For the traybake:

½ tbsp oil

250g plain flour

25g desiccated coconut

2 tsp baking powder

50g butter

150g fat-free yogurt

75g white sugar

2 medium eggs

zest and juice of 2 oranges

For the icing:

100g fat-free yogurt

20g icing sugar (sifted)

10g desiccated coconut

STORING:

This can be kept in an airtight tin (without the icing) at room temperature for up to 2 days. It can be frozen in freezer bags for up to 3 months and defrosted at room temperature in 2 hours.

METHOD

1. Preheat the oven to 180°C Fan/200°C/Gas Mark 6 and use the oil to grease a baking tin approximately 23cm square.

2. Add the flour, desiccated coconut and baking powder to a large bowl and mix well.

3. Melt the butter in a large jug in the microwave. Add the yogurt, sugar and eggs and mix well.

4. Zest and juice the oranges. Hold back 1 teaspoon of the orange zest for the icing but add the rest of the zest and juice to the jug and mix.

5. Pour this mixture into the dry ingredients and mix just enough to combine.

6. Transfer the mixture to the greased baking tin and bake for 22 minutes.

7. Leave to cool for a few minutes before turning the cake out onto a rack to cool completely.

8. Make the icing by mixing the yogurt, icing sugar, desiccated coconut and the reserved orange zest in a small bowl.

9. You can either spread this on top of the cake immediately and cut into twelve slices. Or if you are not intending on eating all the cake straight away, cut the cake up first and add the icing as and when you are serving.

RASPBERRY & WHITE CHOCOLATE COOKIES

| Makes: 15 | Prep time: 10 minutes | Cook time: 15 minutes | Calories: 145 per cookie |

These cookies are brilliant to batch make and keep in the freezer to eat throughout the week. The kids love them in lunchboxes, and I love them with a cup of coffee for an afternoon snack!

INGREDIENTS

125g butter

50g light brown sugar

1 medium egg

1 tsp vanilla extract

100g plain flour

100g porridge oats

¼ tsp bicarbonate of soda

50g raspberry and white chocolate chips mix

STORING:

These cookies can be kept in an airtight tin at room temperature for up to 2 days or frozen in freezer bags for up to 3 months and defrosted at room temperature in 2 hours.

METHOD

1. Preheat the oven to 160°C Fan/180°C/Gas Mark 4 and line two baking trays with parchment paper.

2. Add the butter and sugar to a large bowl and beat with an electric electric hand mixer.

3. Add the egg and vanilla and beat again.

4. Add the flour, oats and bicarbonate of soda and mix with a spoon until all the ingredients are well combined.

5. Finally, add the raspberry and white chocolate chips and mix again.

6. Take one heaped tablespoon of the mixture at a time and add to the lined baking trays.

7. You should be able to make 15 cookies from the mixture.

8. Press down with the back of a spoon and bake in the oven for 15 minutes.

9. The cookies will still be soft when you remove them from the oven. Leave to cool on the baking trays for 10 minutes before transferring to a wire rack to cool completely.

LEMON LOAF

| Makes: 12 slices | Prep time: 7 minutes | Cook time: 35 minutes | Calories: 160 per slice |

Another brilliant batch bake to have on hand during the week. This lemon loaf is light in texture and packed with zesty flavour.

INGREDIENTS

For the loaf cake:

½ tbsp oil

250g plain flour

2 tsp baking powder

50g butter

150g fat-free Greek yogurt

75g white sugar

2 medium eggs

2 lemons

For the glaze:

2 tbsp icing sugar (sifted)

STORING:

This loaf can be kept in an airtight tin at room temperature for up to 2 days or frozen in freezer bags for up to 3 months and defrosted at room temperature in 2 hours.

METHOD

1. Preheat the oven to 180°C Fan/200°C/Gas Mark 6 and use the oil to grease a 680kg (or 1.5lb) loaf tin.

2. Put the flour and baking powder in a large bowl and mix well.

3. Melt the butter in a large jug in the microwave. Add the yogurt, sugar and eggs and mix well.

4. Zest and juice the lemons. Hold back 2 teaspoons of the lemon juice to use to ice the cake but add the rest of the juice and the zest to the jug and mix.

5. Pour this mixture into the dry ingredients and mix just enough to combine.

6. Transfer the mixture to the greased loaf tin and bake for 35 minutes.

7. Leave to cool for a few minutes before turning the cake out onto a rack to cool completely.

8. Make the glaze by mixing the reserved lemon juice with the icing sugar.

7. Pour the glaze over the top of the cake and then cut into twelve slices.

CHOCOLATE POPCORN

| Serves: 4 | Prep time: 2 minutes | Cook time: 5 minutes | Calories: 165 per portion |

Upgrade simple homemade popcorn with a chocolate drizzle. Brilliant for movie nights at home and a super simple and easy one the kids can get involved with, too.

INGREDIENTS

2 tsp oil

100g popcorn kernels

¼ tsp salt

50g milk chocolate

STORING:

This popcorn is best eaten immediately after making, but leftovers will keep in an airtight container at room temperature for up to 2 days.

METHOD

1. Add the oil and popcorn to a large saucepan and mix so that the kernels are all coated in the oil.

2. Add a lid to the saucepan and cook for 4-5 minutes until all the kernels have popped. Shake the saucepan a couple of times.

3. You will know when the kernels have almost all popped as the popping will slow down.

4. At this point turn off the heat and leave the lid on for a minute or two until the popping has completely stopped.

5. Spread the popcorn out onto a large baking tray, removing any unpopped kernels.

6. Mix in the salt and then melt the chocolate in a small bowl in the microwave.

7. Drizzle the melted chocolate over the top of the popcorn and place in the fridge for 5 minutes until the chocolate has hardened.

NOTE:

Popcorn not recommended for children under 4.

CHOCOLATE ORANGE HOT CHOC

| Serves: 4 | Prep time: 1 minute | Cook time: 3 minutes | Calories: 175 per portion |

On a winter's evening, you can't beat a comforting mug of hot chocolate. Skip the shop-bought powder and make your own instead, flavoured with fresh orange!

INGREDIENTS

1 litre semi-skimmed milk

3 tbsp cocoa powder

1 tbsp honey

zest and juice of 1 orange

1 tsp vanilla extract

20g mini marshmallows

STORING:

Leftovers can be kept in the fridge for up to 2 days and reheated in the microwave or on the hob.

METHOD

1. Add the milk, cocoa powder, honey, zest and juice orange and the vanilla to a saucepan on the hob.

2. The orange zest will leave small bits in the hot chocolate. If your kids don't like this, you can pour the hot chocolate through a fine sieve before serving or, alternatively, leave out the zest altogether and just add the orange juice.

3. Whisk until all the ingredients are combined and heat gently for 2-3 minutes. Don't let the milk boil.

4. Pour the hot chocolate into four mugs and top with mini marshmallows.

BANOFFEE MESS

| Serves: 4 | Prep time: 5 minutes | Cook time: none | Calories: 310 per portion |

This dessert is a combination of the classic Eton mess, but with banana and caramel flavours instead. Perfect in the summer for a quick and easy weekend treat.

INGREDIENTS

150ml double cream

200g fat-free Greek yogurt

1 tbsp honey

1 large banana

4 meringue nests

2 tbsp caramel sauce

STORING:

This dessert is best served immediately after making as the meringue will start to dissolve into the cream.

METHOD

1. Add the cream to a large bowl and whip until thick.

2. Add the yogurt and honey and mix well.

3. Cut the banana into slices and break the meringue nests into large bite-sized pieces.

4. Layer the cream mixture in small glasses or jars with the sliced banana and meringue pieces.

5. Drizzle the caramel sauce on top.

6. Serve immediately.

CARROT CAKE MUFFINS

| Makes: 10 | Prep time: 10 minutes | Cook time: 22 minutes | Calories: 175 per muffin |

All the great flavour of carrot cake packed into individual muffins. These are ideal to batch make and keep in the freezer for snacks all week.

INGREDIENTS

200g plain flour

75g porridge oats

1 tsp baking powder

¼ tsp bicarbonate of soda

¼ tsp ground cinnamon

1 medium carrot, finely grated

1 medium red apple, finely grated

30g raisins

50g butter

100g fat-free Greek yogurt

1 medium egg

50g honey

STORING:

These muffins can be kept in an airtight tin at room temperature for up to 2 days. They can be frozen in freezer bags for up to 3 months and defrosted at room temperature in 2 hours.

METHOD

1. Preheat the oven to 180°C Fan/200°C/Gas Mark 6.

2. Put the flour, porridge oats, baking powder, bicarbonate of soda and cinnamon in a large bowl and mix well.

3. Add the grated carrot, grated apple and raisins and mix again.

4. Add the butter to a bowl or jug and melt in the microwave.

5. Mix in the yogurt, egg and honey and then pour this mixture into the dry ingredients.

6. Mix one last time, just enough so that the ingredients are all incorporated.

7. Divide the mixture between 10 silicone muffin cases. I find this easiest to do with an ice-cream scoop. One scoop is the perfect amount of mixture per muffin case.

8. Bake for 20–22 minutes and then leave to cool for a few minutes before removing from the muffin cases to serve.

CHOCOLATE GRANOLA BARS

| Makes: 12 | Prep time: 6 minutes | Cook time: 12 mins, plus 45 mins cooling time | Calories: 140 per bar |

If you're in need of an afternoon chocolate pick-me-up, these granola bars are ideal.
Keep them in the fridge or freezer for grab-and-go snacks to hand.

INGREDIENTS

100g porridge oats

30g Rice Krispies

2 tbsp cocoa powder

70g smooth peanut butter

70g honey

50g butter

25g white chocolate

STORING:

These granola bars can be kept in the fridge for up to 4 days. They can be frozen in freezer bags for up to 2 months and defrosted at room temperature in 2 hours.

METHOD

1. Preheat the oven to 180°C Fan/200°C/Gas Mark 6 and line a square baking dish (approximately 23cm) with parchment paper.

2. Put the porridge oats, Rice Krispies and cocoa powder in a large bowl and mix well.

3. Add the peanut butter, honey and butter to a jug and melt in the microwave. You can also do this in a small saucepan on the hob.

4. Pour the mixture into the bowl and mix well so that all the ingredients are combined.

5. Transfer the mixture into the lined tin and press down with the back of a spoon to make it as compact as possible.

6. Bake for 12 minutes.

7. Once cooked, leave to cool in the tin for about 15 minutes.

8. Melt the white chocolate in the microwave and drizzle this on top.

9. Place the tin into the fridge for 30 minutes to harden.

10. Cut into 12 pieces.

CHOCOLATE MOUSSE

| Serves: 4 | Prep time: 5 minutes | Cook time: minimum 30 mins in fridge | Calories: 160 per portion, incl. toppings |

This dessert tastes super indulgent but is actually relatively healthy, with limited sugar in the ingredients. It's a brilliant dessert to make in advance if you have guests as it will keep in the fridge all day.

INGREDIENTS

4 medium eggs or 130g egg whites from a carton

80g milk chocolate

100g fat-free Greek yogurt

1 tsp vanilla extract

To top:

70g fat-free Greek yogurt

4 strawberries

5g milk chocolate

STORING:

This mousse can be kept in the fridge for 1 day. If making in advance, do not add the yogurt, strawberry and chocolate shaving toppings until ready to serve.

METHOD

1. If using whole eggs, separate the whites from the yolks and add the whites to a large bowl. If you are using a carton of egg whites, pour it straight in.

2. Whisk the egg whites with an electric hand mixer until they are bright white and fluffy.

3. Melt the chocolate in a bowl in the microwave or over a pan of hot water on the hob.

4. Add the yogurt and vanilla to the melted chocolate and mix well.

5. Finally, pour the chocolate mixture into the egg whites and fold just enough to incorporate all the ingredients. You don't want to over-mix it as this will knock all the air out of the mousse.

6. Transfer to four small bowls or ramekins and leave to set in the fridge for a minimum of 30 minutes.

7. When ready to serve, top with more yogurt and chopped strawberries and use a grater to sprinkle with chocolate shavings.

MANGO SORBET

| Serves: 4 | Prep time: 5 minutes | Freezing time: 1 hour | Calories: 75 per portion |

Use bags of supermarket frozen fruit to make this light dessert. Perfect when you want something sweet but healthy too.

INGREDIENTS

400g frozen mango chunks

200ml water

1 tbsp honey

STORING:

Leftover sorbet can be kept in an airtight container in the freezer for up to 2 months. It will need to be left at room temperature for 20–30 minutes or so to defrost before serving.

METHOD

1. Add the frozen mango chunks and water to a powerful blender or food processor and blitz until completely smooth.

2. Add the honey and blitz again.

3. Transfer the mixture to a a 680kg (or 1.5lb) loaf tin and freeze for 1 hour. If you freeze it for longer, you will need to leave it out for 10–15 minutes to defrost a little before serving.

4. Use an ice-cream scoop to make eight scoops of sorbet and serve immediately in four bowls.

AFFOGATO & KIDDIES' AFFOGATO

| Serves: 4 | Prep time: 3 minutes | Cook time: none | Calories: approximately 145 for adult portion (see Note) |

This classic Italian dessert is perfect for days when you fancy a sweet treat after dinner, but don't want to spend a lot of time cooking. The kid-friendly version uses hot chocolate rather than coffee.

INGREDIENTS

8 scoops vanilla ice cream

2 small black coffees

2 small hot chocolates

5g milk chocolate

NOTE:

The calories in this dessert will depend on the type of ice cream that you use. If you use a light ice cream the calories will be about 145 calories per portion. Regular ice cream will obviously be more.

METHOD

1. Add two scoops of vanilla ice cream each to four bowls or glasses.

2. For the adults' portion, pour over the black coffee.

3. For kids, pour over the hot chocolate.

4. Grate the chocolate on top and serve immediately.

INDEX

ACKNOWLEDGEMENTS

Firstly, I want to say a big thank you to everyone who follows me on social media. Whether you have been around since the beginning in 2014 or have just recently found my accounts, your support online has been the catalyst for my cookbooks and I appreciate each and every like, comment and message I receive.

Thank you to the incredible team at Bonnier for turning another one of my small ideas into reality. The work that goes on behind the scenes for over a year to produce a cookbook is immense, and I am so fortunate to yet again have a fantastic team. Thank you to my former editor Beth, my current editor Michelle and her assistant Sophie. And to everyone who worked on the copy-editing, proof-reading, design, production, marketing, publicity and sales.

Thank you to Ella, our photographer; our food stylist, Sophie; and assistant, Louise, for showcasing the recipes with stunning styling and photography. Thank you to Amy for managing to put me at ease and take photos of me when I usually prefer to be at the other side of the camera.

Thank you to my agent, Sarah, for taking a chance on me all those years ago and working so hard to bring another idea to life.

To my family and friends, thank you for all your support and encouragement in the beginning and now. And an extra thank you for those who taste-tasted these recipes on their children!

First published in the UK by Lagom
An imprint of Bonnier Books UK
4th Floor, Victoria House,
Bloomsbury Square,
London, WC1B 4DA

Owned by Bonnier Books
Sveavägen 56, Stockholm, Sweden

Hardback – 978-1-788-707-53-4
Ebook – 978-1-788-707-54-1

A CIP catalogue of this book is available from the British Library.

Designed by EnvyDesign Ltd
Printed and bound in Latvia

1 3 5 7 9 10 8 6 4 2

Recipe and text copyright © Ciara Attwell, 2023
Images on pages 2, 4, 149 © Mooie Fee Photography
All other photos © Ella Miller
Illustrations © Shutterstock
Cover photos © Ella Miller

MIX
Papir | Støtter
ansvarligt skovbrug
FSC® C002795

Lagom is an imprint of Bonnier Books UK
www.bonnierbooks.co.uk

Editor: Beth Eynon

Photographer: Ella Miller

Author photographer: Amy Kolsteren

Assistant Food Stylist: Louise Richardson

Recipe Stylist: Louise Richardson

Copyeditor: Nicky Lovick

Proofreader: Vicky Orchard

Indexer: Kate Inskip

Designer: Graeme Andrew

Cover designer: Studio Polka

CIARA ATTWELL

is an award-winning food blogger and busy mum to two young children. In 2014, she set up her blog, My Fussy Eater, to create meals that catered for the whole family in one go. Ciara's hundreds of thousands of followers find high-quality recipes, easy to understand instructions and helpful tips and tricks on her Facebook, Instagram and YouTube channels. She has worked with Kenwood, Braun and Tesco, and is a brand consultant and children's food expert. Ciara also launched the My Fussy Eater app and Pick Plates, designed to help fussy eater's food habits.

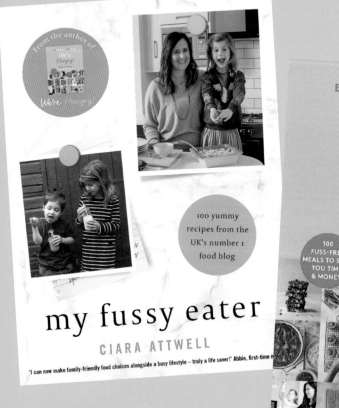